THE GERMAN OPPOSITION

THE GERMAN OPPOSITION TO HITLER

An Assessment

by

HANS ROTHFELS

Translated from the German by
LAWRENCE WILSON

OSWALD WOLFF (PUBLISHERS) LIMITED
London, W.1

FIRST PUBLISHED 1961
FIRST PAPERBACK EDITION 1970
REPRINTED 1973, 1978

Printed in Great Britain by
Lewis Reprints Ltd.
member of Brown Knight & Truscott Group
London and Tonbridge.

CONTENTS

FOREWORD

T HIS study of the German Resistance movement is based in essentials on a public address which was delivered in 1947 at the University of Chicago in memory of 20th July. Being one of the central themes of recent and not only of German history, the subject has preoccupied me ever since. Hence the first undertaking was followed in 1948 by a short book written in English (*The German Opposition to Hitler*, Henry Regnery, Hinsdale, Ill.). This edition contained fairly extensive notes referring to the evidence available at that time and offering a means of checking controversial questions. It was followed in 1949 by a somewhat expanded German edition which was published by the Scherpe-Verlag, Krefeld. Through the years the book appeared to fill a certain gap and as it repeatedly found new readers I was later urged from many sides to prepare a new and revised edition corresponding to the state of our present, greatly extended knowledge. This edition, of which the present book is a translation, was published in the *Fischer Bücherei*, Frankfurt am Main, in 1958. While retaining the original structure of the work, it contained notes which were further expanded to cover the source material which had become known since 1949. With all this it neither was nor is my intention to write a history of the German Resistance, let alone a complete one. My concern throughout is to discuss rather than to narrate, that is, to place the material in certain factual and interpretive contexts with, as an indispensable prerequisite, a basis of fact that shall be as assured as possible.

The book abstains from any kind of Pharisaism, for no one has the right to pass facile judgement on conflicts of conscience and the possibility of unqualified resistance who has not himself fully experienced the trials of life under a totalitarian system. This applies to the standpoint of an author who was only able to observe from the outside the final and most tragic culmination of events that occurred after September, 1939. But the avoidance of exclusive and Pharisaical criteria should not lead to an exaggerated extension of the term "resistance" such as was customary for a time as a form of comfortable self-deception. Though one must recognise the scope of the phenomenon, the varied and diversified character of the Opposition, its numerous degrees and transitions and one must have full sympathy with the more silent forms of resistance expressed in endurance under suffering, in unshakable adherence to convictions or to the rules of decent human conduct, in humanitarian actions and support for the persecuted, it must also be realised that the subject has certain limits.

This applies to all mere criticism of defects or inadequacies in the system, of isolated measures however fateful, of corruption, of tiresome or even infuriating interference in one's personal or professional sphere in so far as this criticism or indignation does not extend sooner or later from the part to the whole and to the basic principles of a criminal régime, compelling action against a government which is leading men and peoples inwardly and outwardly to destruction and is yet the government of one's own country.

This indicates the point at which in peace and even more in war the essential characteristics and the particular dilemma of the German Resistance found expression, a dilemma which distinguishes it both from former revolutions which saw the uprising of an oppressed or underprivileged class and from all insurrectional and freedom-movements, all resistances against a tyranny imposed from without. The way in which very different forms of conscientious thought were applied to the solution of this dilemma must not be simplified or blurred, but must be a main subject of discussion. I think justice can be done to those who remained within the system in order to resist and to the repeated attempts to unite patriotism and opposition on a higher plane and to the effort to distinguish between warning a threatened neutral country and issuing that warning when military attack was imminent —all this can be fairly weighed in the balance as well as religious scruples against an act of violence, against breach of oath and tyrannicide and, above all, the free decision dictated by conscience to take action and an unqualified ethical resolve to ignore the traditional interests of the country and military considerations for the sake of resistance founded on principle. Basically the very conviction that the victory of "the beast from the abyss" was not desirable, indeed even the presentiment that assumed defeat to be the necessary result of *Hubris* led to the same extreme situation. Even a "non-active" opponent like Graf Moltke, who neither speculated on the manner in which the régime would "burn out" nor wished to contribute by direct action to this end, could write to his English friend: "We are ready to help you win the war and the peace."

It is this front beyond the frontiers which beside all other aspects of a profound human and a considerable historical relevance gives to the German opposition to Hitler its special meaning and to the problem of resistance itself its far-reaching and undiminished importance in a world still threatened by totalitarianism.

Tuebingen, March, 1961.   H. R.

FOREWORD TO THE PAPERBACK EDITION

I am glad to know that the English edition of my book which had been out of print for some time, is now being re-issued in a photo-mechanical reproduction. The object of my book was to present students of contemporary history as well as the general reader with a reliable source of information, and the continued demand seems to indicate that this aim was achieved; the student edition may find an even wider audience.

Although a good deal has been written and published on various aspects of anti-Nazi resistance since the book first came out in 1961, neither the structure of my thesis, nor the main facts and their evaluation have, to my mind, been basically affected by new information or discussions of critical issues. German-reading students, however, may like to know that an enlarged and revised edition of my book was published in 1969 ("Die deutsche Opposition gegen Hitler", Neuausgabe. Frankfurt a.M., Fischer-Bücherei No. 1012).

H. R.

Tuebingen, January, 1970.

INTRODUCTION

1. The Basic Character of the Opposition

ANYONE concerned with the problems of the German opposition to Hitler will turn first to the most visible expression of resistance which was manifested in the attempt on the life of the *Führer* on 20th July, 1944. Among those actions which got no further than the planning stage or which were unsuccessful in execution, this was the only one which was actually carried out and nearly reached its goal. Thus the date of 20th July has acquired a kind of symbolical significance. Whatever may be said about the technical or other shortcomings of the plot, its lack of "luck" or the effect of unfavourable circumstances, it should be the historian's first duty to pay tribute to those men who worked for the day of deliverance from tyranny and shame, for an end to the shedding of blood and for the cleansing of the German name and to those many thousands who suffered or died in this cause. Only some few officers were shot on the spot or had an opportunity to put an end to their lives. Most of the victims had to endure interrogation over shorter or longer periods; they were subjected to cross-examination at night which took place under arc-lamps and alternated with direct torture. At the same time they had to reckon with a threat to their wives and children which often enough became reality. It is said to have been a recognised rule in the French Resistance that nobody could be expected to withstand the methods used by the Gestapo for extorting confessions for longer than twenty-four hours. If a prisoner managed to shield his fellow-conspirators for that length of time, they might meanwhile have found means of ensuring their safety.

If one applies this criterion, which indeed implies above-average courage and endurance, to the men and women who were held in solitary confinement in the Gestapo cellars in the Prinz-Albrecht-Strasse or elsewhere, often in holes too narrow to sit down in, their steadfastness alone stands out as a testimonial of historic significance. This summary tribute must suffice. The

Gestapo reports on the results of interrogations have so far been only partially assessed and they have their own problems as source material. But considering the fact that upwards of 7,000 people were arrested after 20th July and assuming that some of them made forced confessions while others who were subsequently caught in the Gestapo dragnet in the so-called *Gewitteraktion* had nothing to do with the plot, the results of the interrogations are extraordinarily scanty. Though the discovery of incriminating documents opened up many lines of inquiry, the fortitude of those with knowledge of at least one or other sector of the opposition front prevented the Gestapo from ever becoming aware of the full extent of the Resistance. Moreover, many of those who fell directly or indirectly as victims of 20th July withstood the final test with a bearing which was memorable in the general human sense, whatever the political implications of their plans or their significance in this, the darkest phase of German history. During the course of the trials some of the accused appeared more as prosecutors than as indicted criminals. They accepted martyrdom as an honour, as their contribution to the realisation of brother-hood among men. And the consciousness of dying for a cause extending beyond their own lives remained unshaken on the very brink of an ignominious death. As he was being led to the gallows, the Jesuit Father Delp said smiling to the Catholic prison chap-lain : "In a few minutes I shall know more than you." Poelchau, the Lutheran pastor in Tegel who was himself an active member of the Opposition, has testified to the same other-wordliness on the part of the men to whom he gave spiritual comfort. Among the farewell letters from prison, too, of which many have been preserved, not a few touch on the ultimate questions of human existence and some are classics among human documents.

From these few facts alone a provisional and very general con-clusion may be drawn : no assessment of the German opposition to Hitler will be adequate which clings to the limited sphere of political considerations and possibilities, which inquires, for in-stance, into the "class" motives of the "old Elite" who were so strongly represented in the conspiracy, thus adopting of supposed necessity certain methods of sociological analysis, or which stresses in the main the "national" aims of the Resistance and judges them in the last resort by the criterion of their outward success or failure. Such so-called "realistic" interpretations are justified in so far as the material evidence lies within their field. But to reach the deeper springs one must try to get at the prime movers, those forces of moral self-affirmation which go far beyond considerations of mere political necessity. From a knowledge of many of the participants, Ernst Jünger wrote in his diary in the spring of 1944 : "One can see, too, that it is the moral substance, not the political which spurs to action." Certainly, the ethical and religious impulses of the Resistance were not alive only in Germany, but here they had to be expressed under the pressure of unexampled circumstances in an exemplary way. To this basic analysis of the conflict Graf Moltke subscribed when, a few days before his execution, he wrote to his wife that one thought only remained, the thought of Christianity as the "sheet-anchor" in time of chaos.

But this bed-rock appears not only in connection with the events of 20th July. A further very striking example is provided by the Scholls, brother and sister, and by their friends. We know enough today about the students' revolt in Munich in February, 1943, to see in it more than a mere consequence of the catastrophe of Stalingrad or of an exceptionally provocative speech by the *Gauleiter* of Upper Bavaria. The Munich students Hans and Sophie Scholl had been at war with the Party since their secondary school days; at the university they belonged to a group which conducted a pamphlet campaign with the "White Rose" letters. The group had connections with the Catholic periodical *Hochland*, with the Catholic writer Theodor Haecker and with other universities. And yet the Munich students can hardly have believed that a spontaneous rising on their part could alone alter the course of events. They were, on the other hand, firmly convinced of something else, of the necessity of bearing witness to their faith and of clearing themselves as well as the name of Germany. "Is it not a fact", asks one of the pamphlets, "that today every decent German is ashamed of his government?" Thus the manifesto of 18th February, 1943, called on the youth of Germany to "avenge and atone" so that it could contribute to the building of "a new spiritual Europe". In the pamphlets, too, which Hans Scholl and his friends wrote or distributed, a metaphysical tone is not lacking. "Everywhere and in all ages", one of them states, "the demons have been waiting in darkness for the hour in which man would weaken, when of his own volition he would abandon his place in the order of things founded for him by God on freedom, surrender to the pressure of Evil, detach himself from the Powers of a higher order and so, having taken the first step voluntarily, be driven to the second and third and ever further steps with frenzied speed." It was in the same attitude of mind that Kurt Huber, who amongst the professors of the university fostered this group and shared execution with five of their number, wrote in his last letter that death was to be the "fair copy" of his life. And on the walls of many Munich houses appeared the inscription : "The spirit lives."

It seems an obvious assumption that the resistance group which had one of its centres in Goering's Air Ministry and has become known as the "Red Chapel" was, as it were, of a more "realistic" colour. And in fact it is beyond question that some of its members were at least in continual contact with the Russians and, until their secret service was uncovered in August, 1942, supplied them by radio with military information. That fact should in no way be glossed over. But a summary dismissal of these men and women as mere agents of the Kremlin and therefore no true members of the genuine Opposition is equally unjustified. We shall return to the problem of high treason. Here it should be noted that no clear line can really be drawn after the event between actions serving the "salvation" of the country and those serving its "surrender". Neither is it appropriate to think into the situations then prevailing the perspectives and experiences of a satellite existence. Men like Schulze-Boysen and Arvid Harnack were not true to the "Party line". They remained unaffected by the episode of the Hitler-Stalin pact for the very reason that they were grounded in an idealistic and independent Communism. Like another member of their circle, the poet Adam Kuckhoff, they were concerned with "resistance from the spirit". Though their aims and methods differed from those of other groups, their mental and practical attitudes did not. Of Arvid Harnack, even the prosecutor Roeder, who was a notorious blood-hound, said : "He died like a man." And Schulze-Boysen wrote to his parents : "In Europe it is after all the custom for spiritual seed to be sown with blood."

Beside these selected and particularly dramatic examples, there are innumerable others of courage, self-sacrifice and martyrdom. Of course, not everyone who deserted from the war can claim noble motives. Similarly, those who, because of some chance expression of criticism or indignation, incurred the death penalty as defeatist elements or for their destructive influence on national morale cannot for that reason be included in the Resistance.

There should be no misunderstanding on that point. But the fact that this criticism existed and that a considerable part of the National Socialist machinery—in the years 1943-45, the Gestapo alone numbered more than 40,000 men—was occupied in neutralising or in keeping under lock and key an equally considerable portion of the German people, indeed, the fact that bit by bit a whole army of Party functionaries and security forces were tied down by this task should not be forgotten. According to an SS document there were 21,400 persons interned at the beginning of the war. But this figure gives no indication of how many people had by then passed through concentration camps or died behind barbed wire. The estimates given by German emigrants range between 750,000 and 1,200,000 and of these political prisoners are estimated at between 500,000 and 600,000. Death sentences for political reasons have been given as 12,000.

Whatever more detailed research may reveal, no responsible assessment of the German opposition to Hitler can overlook the brutal language of such figures. They give some indication of the scope of passive or active resistance offered by nameless thousands, however varied the immediate causes of their arrests may have been. The young people in the "Edelweiss" groups or in the "Packs" were more deeply involved in the Resistance and in the sacrifices which it demanded than is generally known. It is reported, for instance, that in Krefeld at least 30 per cent of the Hitler Youth were secret members of the "Edelweiss". The concentration camp in Neuwied (April, 1944) was intended solely for boys under twenty. Giving evidence in court in 1939, a Gestapo agent stated that "at least 2,000 boys and girls" were organised in the "Pack" in the whole of Germany.

Further, the intellectuals and artists of the so-called "internal emigration" should be remembered who kept the fires burning with much greater success than observers beyond the frontiers believed, also the men and women who had the courage to help their Jewish friends and neighbours by hiding them and giving them food, obtained forged papers for them or who built up a secret transport system for persons wanted by the Gestapo. Chapter and verse for all these activities of an oppositional nature can be supplied, and some require detailed discussion. But above all they need to be set in the total picture and this must be related to the background of conditions and possibilities that existed in Germany. We must, in particular, concern ourselves with the inner meaning of the German Opposition movement, as far as possible without preference for any special group, in its manifold forms, in its nature and its extent, in its composition and aims, in the main branches of its activities both inside and outside Germany. Only so can the way be prepared for an assessment of the essential aspects of the historical facts.

2. Obstacles on the Road to Truth

But first the difficulties must be realised which such an attempt inevitably encountered, particularly abroad, in the years following the end of the war. This is not merely a matter of reviewing the ground covered, for much as the situation has changed—to a degree in which the "obstacles on the road to truth" appear to be greater now inside Germany than outside—we are not dealing here with prejudices that have been overcome. Moreover, their discussion will lead us back from another direction to the basic characteristics of the Opposition.

We must start with the thesis that prevailed throughout the war and at its conclusion, at least in former enemy countries, to the effect that no opposition to Hitler worth speaking of ever existed. The conviction was held that as a political nation the Germans differed from all other peoples, for they had, it was believed, voluntarily associated themselves with or submitted out of cowardice to the tyrannical rule of criminals, either through innate wickedness, or from an acquired habit of blind obedience, or under the influence of some specifically baneful philosophy. It was assumed that they, that is, the whole nation had deliberately shut their eyes to terrible crimes which had been committed by Germans. And the way in which the inescapable evidence of a counter-movement leading up to the attempt on Hitler's life was interpreted was in exact conformity with these views. Opposition only began, it was believed, when, confronted with defeat, the "Prussian generals" attempted to save their own lives—and preserve the General Staff for a third world war.

This misinterpretation can partly be explained by objective difficulties which stood in the path of truth. A movement opposing a terroristic and to a great extent totalitarian system works under conditions which are past the comprehension of anyone who has not actually lived in a police state of that kind. To adopt an oppositional attitude, let alone to give public expression to it, required not only a kind of personal heroism which appears to have become a rare phenomenon in all countries under modern social conditions, but which entailed a most serious threat to family and friends. Few foreigners were prepared, particularly in wartime, to realise that Germany after 1933 was an occupied country. Admittedly, conditions there differed very greatly from those prevailing in other countries which later succumbed to this fate. In Germany there was none of that aura of glory which deservedly surrounds a resistance movement opposing a foreign conqueror or a tyranny imposed from without. By contrast the German Opposition was obliged, particularly in later years, to adopt a camouflage (it did so to a lesser extent than might be imagined) and to give itself that appearance of inactivity which probably deceived a large number of Germans just as it gave a false picture to the public in Great Britain and the United States. The slightest mention of names or dates in underground propaganda or over the foreign radio could spell disaster. This danger was naturally more acute after the outbreak of war which inevitably exposed any form of opposition to the charge of treason and put opponents of the régime more or less consciously in the position of having to abandon patriotic considerations of a traditional kind. In addition, there was the continual displacement of the population in wartime and the effect of bombing attacks which hit opponents and supporters of the régime alike. Both could lead to a disruption of existing resistance cells and a spread of apathy.

Thus there were many reasons for a deceptive picture of a calm and monolithically compact nation. Moreover, the Intelligence and Counter-Espionage Department of the Combined General Staff, in which service some of the most active members of the Opposition were to be found, wisely took care that the protective veil should remain intact and as far as possible covered the leading members of the conspiracy.

But this alone does not explain the extent and persistence of the prevailing errors. Rather, there were many factors other than those objective ones arising from the situation which contributed to the misunderstanding which was so widespread in foreign countries. This was in part due to entirely human reactions which were expressed as indifference or partisanship. Of course, everyone was in a position to know or find out that before the seizure of power the National Socialists never polled more than 37 per cent of the total votes (July, 1932), that in November, 1932, when the economic position seemed to be improving slightly this figure sank to 32 per cent, and that in March, 1933, at the manipulated and hysterical elections which followed the Reichstag fire it only rose to 44 per cent. But who, in the great public outside Germany, bore these facts in mind? On the other hand, it was known throughout the world that a wave of persecution had passed over Germany since the beginning of 1933 and that those from whom the most energetic resistance might have been expected had been taken into "protective custody" or forced to flee the country. But so long as the inmates of concentration camps consisted entirely of Germans, the atrocities committed in them received little notice abroad. When the *Brown Book of the Hitler Terror*, which sought to draw attention to these misdeeds, was published by Alfred Knopf in New York, it was reviewed in the *New York Times* by no less a person than the former American Ambassador to Berlin, James W. Gerard. Confronted with the revelations contained in the book he thought it proper to write: "Hitler is doing much for Germany, his unification of the Germans, his destruction of Communism, his training of the young, his creation of a Spartan state animated by patriotism, his curbing of parliamentary government, so unsuited to the German character, his protection of the rights of private property are all good." When Germans who had fled from their homeland told their British or American friends of their own or their friends' experiences in Buchenwald, Oranienburg or Dachau they encountered, as often as not, incredulity and this increased when they came to mention the numbers imprisoned or the methods used in concentration camps.

Of course this attitude underwent a basic change in the spring of 1945. The unspeakable horrors which came to light in camps as they were freed and the evidence unearthed of crimes committed in Poland and Russia released a storm of indignation in the western world. Indeed, the discoveries even exceeded the expectations of those who were best informed on National Socialist methods. But when proof of "German bestiality" emerged, little was said of the great numbers of Germans who had been among the victims. Victor Gollancz, the editor of the *Brown Book* of 1933 and an author who, as few others, has fought injustice wherever and in whatever form it appeared, did not fail to draw attention to this oversight. Writing in retrospect of the "outcry which deafened us at the time of the Buchenwald revelations", he stated that they were no revelation to those "who had continually tried since 1933 to arouse an indolent and sceptical public and speak for men and women who suffered unspeakable tortures in these camps."

There is no question that the attitude of comfortable disregard which Gollancz stigmatised not only continued so far as German victims of concentration camps were concerned, but was systematically fostered by official silence. For years the American public was not officially informed that up to the summer of 1943 there were practically no foreigners in Buchenwald and that among the 20,000 survivors (as compared with 51,000 deaths) there were still more than 2,000 Germans. And only a very rough picture has been given of the composition according to nationality of the guards. No attempt has been made, for instance, to extract details from the documents in the possession of the Western allies, concerning the number of foreigners in the special "Death's Head" formations or in the other SS units which "took care" of the concentration camps.

Yet for those interested in a more balanced picture there is no lack—and there was no lack, even ten years ago—of documentary evidence proving the existence of such a "Black Internationale". It is known, for instance, that Croats and Ukrainians were among those guarding German camps and that so-called "Protective Corps" were formed of Lithuanians, Latvians and Estonians whose members had to "look after" their own countrymen. For the fulfilment of these tasks in occupied countries a similar type of individual apparently offered himself or could be found as in Germany. Thus numerous Dutchmen have been accused of torturing their countrymen and in the notorious camp at Gurs, which existed before the Vichy era and was always administered exclusively by Frenchmen, the death-rate was hardly less than in "normal" German camps. That this was, in fact, an "Internationale" has been testified in striking manner by a Swiss journalist who did a tour of inspection through South-West Germany at the invitation of General Lattre de Tassigny. He reported that the French uncovered a typical horror camp in their zone of occupation, but on closer examination a considerable part of the guard company proved to consist of French *miliciens*.

It is understandable that no revelations have ever been made about this camp. They would have too obviously run counter to the official line of propaganda. While all available evidence and the results of any sober examination are calculated to show that modern mass civilisation generates a reservoir of evil forces whose release spells naked barbarism and while it should similarly be clear that potential torturers as well as martyrs are present in every nation, a policy of hate and revenge has decreed that this should be overlooked. This has happened as a consequence of total war, but also as a result of the picture of the "eternal" German propagated in the main by Vansittart and underlying the Morgenthau Plan. Did not General Eisenhower himself support such views when he characterised the entire German population as "synthetic paranoid"? Thus the attempt was made—certainly with the incidental object of maintaining the "morale" and "security" of the occupation troops—to contend that there are no "good Germans" except dead ones (a saying first coined in the United States during the wars with the Red Indians) and that bestiality was the specific characteristic of so degenerate a people.

We are not concerned here to correct this distorted picture—which in any case hardly persists now—and still less to make a counter-attack with reference, for instance, to the widespread bestiality that occurred in Eastern Germany after the collapse. The phrase "to be quits" is one of the most dubious and nihilistic of our time. But we are certainly concerned to see justice done to a nation against which discrimination has been collectively exercised and still more to the human factors in a borderline situation such as resistance in a totalitarian State expresses. The continuing demands which such a historical phenomenon contains are equally our concern. The way to this realisation has been a difficult one. There were enough people, and in allied countries as well, who knew the truth or a part of the truth, but at first they were unable to voice it. In particular, there is evidence to show that the intelligence services of the Western allies had a very clear picture of what was happening in wartime Germany. That was the case even before Allen Welsh Dulles took control of the Office of Strategic Services (O.S.S.) on the Continent and, from November, 1942, onwards, maintained continual contact with the German underground movement from Switzerland. There is also no doubt that the leading politicians and diplomats in Britain and the United States were informed in detail of the structure and aims of the German Opposition movement and that they were aware of its extension from the Right to the extreme Left, of the leading personalities in the Civil Service and the Officers' Corps who were involved in it and of the participation of the Churches as well as that of the trade unions.

On can well understand that this insight into realities and the facts on which it was founded were guarded as top secret so long as the outcome of the war remained undecided and Hitler's position seemed still unshaken. It is harder to understand why the official radio announcement from Washington on the evening of 20th July repeated Hitler's lie about the "small clique of ambitious officers" and even enlarged on it. And the same line of propaganda was continued after the end of hostilities. An attempt was made to belittle the importance of evidence which had meanwhile come to light and to present the conspiracy against Hitler as the concern of an aristocratic clique or a "club" of hopelessly outdated and anachronistic aristocrats. One may admit that, misleading though they were, such interpretations represented an advance on the phase of complete silence. For a considerable time, the German Opposition was taboo. But then some former members of the U.S. Intelligence Service raised their voices against this silence and with their knowledge of the facts helped the truth on its way. First of these was a former officer of the Naval Intelligence Service, Alexander B. Maley, who in February, 1946, wrote an article entitled : "The Epic of the German Underground Movement." He was followed by Franklin L. Ford, a former Army officer who had been attached for special duties to the O.S.S. In July, 1946, he published an article : "The 20th July in the History of the German Resistance." Then Allen Welsh Dulles, whose key position has already been mentioned, supplied comprehensive information in his book, *Conspiracy in Germany*. Finally, the Occupation Authorities allowed articles to be published on the subject and in 1947, admittedly from Switzerland, Rudolf Pechel published his book, *German Resistance*. In the following decade much devoted research was done and an enormous quantity of material published under titles with which we do not propose to burden this account.

But it cannot be said that the old prejudices have completely vanished. Their effects are strongly evident in British historiography, for instance in L. B. Namier's studies and in J. W. Wheeler-Bennett's book *The Nemesis of Power*. These authors still harbour the suspicion that the activities of the Opposition were based on ill-concealed nationalism or narrow group aims and did not represent a real rupture of, in fact, extremely strong traditional attachments and therefore all the more, because of this conflict, action based on conscience. While the attitude, whether real or read into events, of the "patriot" or the "believer in the State" appears in this context as a reproach, in some internal German attacks which are made today the situation is reversed. There are those who do not see, as people abroad once did, the catastrophic development that has taken place as founded on the basic evil of German docility towards a criminal *Führer*, but on a different basic evil, that of "German discord". The reproach levelled at Hitler then becomes confined to the fact that he did not stamp on the head of this "noxious worm" in good time. This and other forms of attack go to confirm that the theme of the Resistance is not outmoded but extremely topical and that it concerns criteria of ethical as well as political action which in the circumstances of our time with its ideological fronts have gained a new actuality extending beyond national frontiers.

CONDITIONS AND POSSIBILITIES

1. German "Submissiveness"

OUR study is concerned with problems of opposition to a totalitarian régime, that is, with problems that do not effect one country only, and accordingly with historical facts that are relevant to the basic theses of resistance. It is therefore not intended to trace the oft discussed (and overstressed) "spiritual ancestry" of National Socialism or the forms and causes of its rise. In particular, there can be no place for a discussion of the complex theme of the collapse of the Weimar Republic, the problem of what has been called the "decay of power" or for a detailed examination of the events which led to the Nazi seizure of power. Briefly it may be said that very particular conditions of German public life were involved in this disastrous development and individual actions in fateful combination with very general politico-social circumstances, the consequences of the first world war and the Versailles Treaty as well as with those of the inflation and a world-wide depression. Moreover, the way to catastrophe was prepared by a decline in creative and religious forces and a cultural and moral crisis which was not confined to Germany and for which the Swiss, Max Picard, has found a pregnant formula with his book entitled *Hitler in Ourselves.*

All this should not be misunderstood as an attempt to excuse what happened in Germany. There is no reason to show indulgence towards ruffians and terrorists or to careerists and those who sought advancement from the revolution and tried to climb on the band-waggon. Neither are the widespread phenomena of cowardice and mass hysteria a mitigating circumstance. Neither do the members of the upper classes in Germany who succumbed to a Fascist ideology, that is, to the same class-conditioned self-deception apparent in the words of James W. Gerárd already quoted and in those of many other foreigners deserve pity on the grounds that a rude awakening awaited them.

It can be stated as a fact that very few people possessed a clear insight into the events which resulted in the rise of National Socialism. And even today this avalanche, this bursting of the dam appears to far too many observers as a kind of normal revolution in the style of the nineteenth century. From this view there follows a tendency to see also the opposition movements in a false light. People are content to judge by the same criteria as are normally applied to the political upheavals of a former epoch. Questions are asked about the class structure or party affiliation of the oppositional elements, and the basic significance of the Opposition as a whole, which may be defined as the Human against the Sub-human, is too easily overlooked. What triumphed after the pseudo-legal revolution of 1933 was in fact and to a great extent the dark forces forming the sediment of every modern society. It has been rightly said that they seized power by a surprise flank attack carried out in the main by declassed individuals. They found their numerically broadest support amongst the unemployed and the impoverished *petite bourgeoisie,* that is, in a social no-man's-land. But after the dominance of an energetic and fanatical minority had been firmly established the circumstances surrounding the seizure of power changed to those of its maintenance which of course were of a widely different character.

Certainly no one even moderately familiar with totalitarian methods and practices will be tempted to consider the 100 per cent plebiscites in favour of Hitler as genuine expressions of support. Yet there can be no doubt about the widespread effectiveness of that diabolical mixture of terror and propaganda which was characteristic of the National Socialist régime. And it was not only fear of the overt or concealed weapons of the régime, of the rubber truncheon or the block superviser which provoked a race to join the Party or its affiliated organisations. To a great extent it was the necessity of economic existence which since the inflation had been reduced to bare subsistence. And reinforcing these motives there was undeniably an emotional urge played upon in masterly fashion by the instruments of propaganda, a sham-idealistic attraction or the chimera of the national community (*Volksgemeinschaft*) which cast a spell, particularly on young people. In the beginning also an apparent improvement in social conditions, particularly the artificial reduction of unemployment, placed a psychological trump-card in the hands of the régime, and the same applied in later years to Hitler's success in foreign policy.

The fact that Hitler's admirers abroad and those who sought peace at any price contributed considerably to the victory of the methods of a well-calculated mass psychology in no way alters the symptomatic significance of this propaganda success. All the same, the men of the German Opposition were entitled to look on this support from outside as a real stab in the back. Even a man with the political insight of a Winston Churchill spoke of Hitler in 1935 with admiration for "the courage, the perseverance and the vital force which enabled him to challenge, defy, conciliate or overcome all the authorities or resistance which barred his path". Long after he had become an opponent of the appeasement policy, as late as November, 1938, Churchill echoed this admiration, though with the deliberate object at the time of exerting a tranquillising effect. According to *The Times* of 7th November, 1938, he stated: "I have always said that if Great Britain were defeated in war I hoped we should find a Hitler to lead us back to our rightful position among the nations." But then Churchill added: "I am sorry that he has not been mellowed by the great success that has attended him." But the question, to what extent and for what reasons Hitler's régime was applauded abroad is not a subject of this study. What matters here is that masses of Germans enthusiastically applauded or obediently supported a system of government and national leaders of whose criminal character no doubt could exist, at least not after the first eighteen months of the régime and the blood-bath of 30th June, 1934. It must be added that even those who performed only lip-service were often enough caught in a net of concessions and lies which inevitably had an emasculating effect.

It is a frequently discussed question whether this moral land-slide can be attributed to constitutional weaknesses in the German character or to a kind of "growth disturbance" in German political development. Was it not, as the more extreme thesis maintains, the result of disastrous tendencies evident in the whole course of German history, or at least since Luther, Frederick the Great and Bismarck? Such questions have often been asked and answered in the affirmative in books and controversial writings with more or less one-sidedness. Not all these publications belong to propaganda literature or are a mere expression of Vansittartism. But whoever throws stones from a feeling of moral superiority should first be prepared to examine carefully his own conscience or try to find an adequate testing ground. It is comparatively simple and may often enough be pharisaical to pass judgement never having undergone experiences comparable to those of the Germans after 1933 or if one has oneself, perhaps in small things and without realising it, failed no less miserably than many Germans did.

Of a very different character are many of the writings in which Germans themselves took up the question in the first years after the war how it was possible for a highly civilised people to submit to a criminal régime. This has led to strongly critical examinations of certain political and social, spiritual and religious characteristics of the German tradition and to questioning at a deeper level. "The real problem", wrote a Jesuit priest, "is not Hitler, but the possibility of being infected by Hitler." Or in the words of Karl Jaspers : "We must try to recognise the seed of the evil which was planted a long time ago."

It hardly needs saying that this critical self-examination differs in the most favourable way from the attitude of those who, in 1945, suddenly discovered that they had never been National Socialists. To be aware of personal responsibility for what one does or omits to do and to sweep one's own back-yard is in fact a necessary part of any thorough house cleansing. Or, as the Catholic poet Reinhold Schneider has said : "When the name of a family or a nation is indicted every single member is called upon to strive for a new and purer dignity." Such self-examination and such a demand leave the question of political or juridical guilt far behind, raising in their place into full clarity the metaphysical and religious nature of the problem of responsibility. In anticipation it may be said here that this attitude corresponds precisely with that adopted by leading men of the German Opposition movement. Long before they had to face the defeat of Germany, they followed the dictates of their aroused conscience. They recognised their personal responsibility for crimes committed in the name of Germany and they undertook to atone for them by deeds or sacrifice. This was indeed an awareness of sin which went much deeper than any conception of faulty historical development.

But even if it is correct (and there is much to be said for this thesis) that uncertainty in the traditions and the moral structure of German social life, or lack of education in individual initiative or civic self-confidence facilitated the acceptance of a tyrannical system, the danger of inappropriate generalisation remains. In fact, the question of the degree of German submissiveness has been obscured by a good deal of begging the question. It is not possible to reach a valid judgement leaving out of account the fact of brute force, whether this was confined to threats or took the form of actual maltreatment and torture. Hundreds of thousands "submitted" because they were defenceless and without legal remedy, not because they felt attracted by the system or expected material advantage from it. If, bearing in mind the continual menace of the rubber truncheon, one reviews the weaknesses held to be typically German, there is more cause for surprise at the *limitation* than the *extent* of submissiveness. In fact, it can be said that the Opposition was more widespread and to a greater extent one of principle than generally held views about the character of the German people or knowledge of totalitarian dynamism would suggest. Indeed, the assertion will be made and more closely substantiated that, in view of the unparalleled difficulties confronting it and of its basic orientation towards human integrity and goals confined neither to a single country or class, the German Opposition to Hitler has gained a political significance extending far beyond that of a purely national or social freedom movement.

2. *Degrees of Non-conformity*

During the Third Reich the German people can be said to have fallen into four rough groups : actual Nazis, nominal Nazis, non-Nazis and anti-Nazis. Obviously it is impossible to define precisely the relations of these groups to one another; over the years the dividing lines must have frequently changed and one group must have merged into another. When the American Military Government checked over one million applicants for employment in the U.S. Zone, it was found that in 50 per cent of the cases there was "no evidence of Nazi activity". Certainly, in the light of experience with Military Government questionnaires doubts regarding the accuracy of such negative statements are highly justified, particularly in view of their context. They may represent a good deal of successful camouflage, for this was an art in which a very thorough schooling had been obtained during the Hitler period and Germans required no "re-education" to continue its practice after 1945. But even allowing for this source of error, the percentage of non-Nazis remains surprisingly high. It may be assumed that the figure of 50 per cent merges in imperceptible stages into that of nominal Nazis. Further, the complaint of von Schlabrendorff against non-Nazis may be remembered. "Their lack of character", he states, "gave us more trouble than the arbitrariness and brutality of the Nazis."

In truth the problem of such an amorphous and only negatively characterised group is extremely complicated. The same phenomenon occurs in all totalitarian states. It must be no less apparent in the Soviet Union than under other dictatorships and would deserve more thorough research. Among the non-Nazis in Germany there were certainly many who pursued the policy of the ostrich and whose characteristic attitude of tepid neutrality made a convinced Party member seem attractive in comparison. But the same group included that very numerous element that can be termed "the silent Opposition". And this phenomenon must be measured by the total claim of the prevailing system over all forms, even the most private, of civil life. In theory, at any rate, this claim was more comprehensive in Germany than anywhere else and it found classic expression in Dr. Ley's bombastic statement: "In National Socialist Germany such a thing as a private individual does not exist." Taking this into account it becomes clear that to show "no evidence of Nazi activity" was in itself a type of opposition, or rather, a potential form of resistance.

Such an attitude of abstention was not without danger, though this could be mitigated by unobtrusiveness. It was therefore easier for anonymous men and women to belong to the silent Opposition than for prominent people or those who in some capacity stood in the limelight. But the significance of the phenomenon should not be underestimated. It shows a reserve of forces which the active Resistance could count on at the moment when power had been struck from the hand of the oppressors. At all events, this "reserve front" leads one to suppose that, after their fashion, wide sections of the population showed themselves impervious to indoctrination. They did not depart in the ordinary things of daily life from the dictates of human decency. Though making the indispensable minimum of concessions, they remained morally unaffected. They did not accept the régime as a permanent state of affairs and they never ceased to hope for its end, though they well knew that they could not revolt against the Gestapo with their bare hands.

Admittedly, this demeanour eludes precise definition, but in many cases it could be observed with surprising clarity. In factories and offices the subject of conversation would automatically change as soon as Party members, whose identity was always well known, or informers were out of earshot. Between non-Nazis there was a silent, at times almost a mysterious understanding. It found audible expression in only one form : the caustic jokes at the expense of the régime which spread like wildfire. When occasionally the Nazis thought it advisable to open a safety-valve by permitting an uncensored edition of the Munich Fasching newspaper, *Blaueste Nachrichten*, they must have been unpleasantly surprised, not only by the contents of the paper, but by the speed of its distribution throughout the whole of Germany.

Another striking characteristic of the "silent Opposition" was the numerical increase of small circles which discussed philosophical, religious, artistic or international problems. This form of "separatism" could also prove dangerous at times and could result one day in the dreaded ringing of the front door-bell at five in the morning. Indeed, the group of non-Nazis merged equally into anti-Nazis and nominal Party adherents. When Mussolini visited Berlin in 1937 and Graf Moltke refused to decorate the windows of his Unter den Linden office in the usual manner, persuading other tenants of the building to refrain also, something more was certainly apparent than "no evidence of Nazi activity" on the house-front.

No less does the group of nominal Nazis evade schematic judgement. Egoistic and idealistic motives were often inextricably interwoven in the attitude of those who "went along" with the Party. It can be said that there was no more dangerous misapprehension than the belief that by co-operating with or joining the Party excesses could be alleviated and "worse prevented". In the whole context and broadly speaking, this belief was undoubtedly wrong. And often it was no more than a means of comfortable self-deception. In retrospect many observers consider that without the co-operation and technical knowledge of officials, factory managers and other trained personnel a collapse in the administration and economy of the National Socialist régime would have taken place, possibly at a very early stage. Further, it is arguable that technicians and highly specialised experts took a particular responsibility on themselves by accepting in the abstract, as it were, demands for maximum effort while professing to hold no responsibility for its underlying purpose.

But the much discussed problem of "staying on the job" which as a question of conscience pervades, for instance, the memoirs of Secretary of State von Weizsäcker, cannot be disposed of by such reflections. There were men who, with their eyes wide open and foreseeing their participation in defeat, humbled themselves to take office or join the Party for the sole reason that opposition could only be built up from the inside. And it is clear that some of those who remained in high positions and "went along" with the Party not only preserved their inner independence, but sooner or later took part with varying degrees of determination in the Resistance.

Several of them were or became members of the active Opposition. They worked effectively under the cloak of their membership of the ruling caste and even under the protection of a high position in the Gestapo or the SS. But beside these extreme cases there was another very important though less tangible phenomenon. In the technical branches of the Civil Service the number of non-Party members remained relatively high. Here, too, nominal Nazis who were superficial conformists were often able successfully to maintain "anachronistic" principles of professional ethics. Not a few men and women who escaped persecution and terror owed their lives to this fact or found sympathy and help in highly unexpected quarters. There is no doubt that, though the Civil Service as a whole was forced to toe the Party line, there were entire groups within it in silent but effective opposition and that they opened emergency exits wherever they could.

This has been recognised in a supplement to the official American report on the effects of aerial bombardment which was published in 1947. Under the heading "German Morale" the report states: "Quietly working within the confines of the machine, there were elements opposing National Socialism. As far as the police were concerned, it is clear that the detective force contained substantial numbers of the old supporters of the Republic who had mainly belonged to the Social Democratic party. Such men might go so far as to arrange escapes for intended victims of the Gestapo by entering their names in the missing persons files, after having warned them of an impending arrest. It was known to 'insiders' that there were quite active cells of this nature in government agencies, such as the Ministry of the Interior, the Ministry of Justice, the Ministry of Labour, and certain courts and prose-cutors' offices, not to mention local government services. Such persons could, and sometimes did, effectively sabotage Nazi law enforcement."

3. Attitude to Jews

In the framework of a silent Opposition which organised resis-tance and sabotage of this kind, the attitude of the German people towards the persecuted Jews requires particular attention. It is unnecessary to stress that anti-Semitism was a primitive element in the National Socialist movement on the basis of a ten-dentious racial theory, but also in connection with anti-Capitalism or anti-Communism, or that it had a strong attraction for broad sections of the population and opened the door to the worst ex-cesses as well as odious personal enrichment. But that these atti-tudes and actions enjoyed more or less general approval or were willingly tolerated is in no way the case. A White Book on the "Treatment of German Nationals in Germany" published by the British Government after the outbreak of war contained letters from Germans giving expression to the indignation which was certainly present in wide sections of the population after the so-called "spontaneous" pogroms of 9th November, 1938. No less interesting is the report of the British Consul General in Frankfurt who wrote on 14th December, 1938 : "It seems to me that mass sexual perversity may offer an explanation for this otherwise inexplicable outbreak. I am persuaded that, if the Government of Germany depended on the suffrage of the people, those in power and responsible for these outrages would be swept away by a storm of indignation if not put up against a wall and shot."

It may be that this British observer was too optimistic. And certainly the German official went too far who wrote to another Englishman that "the German people had nothing whatever to do with these disturbances". All the same, it should be remem-bered that while Goebbels was proclaiming them to be a spon-taneous reaction of the German people to the murder of Herr von Rath, the supreme Party court of judicature was reporting to Goering : "Down to the last man the public knows that political actions like that of 9th November are organised and carried out by the Party, whether this is admitted or not." Further, an SS *Brigadeführer's* admission in a letter to Himmler is not without interest: "Indigenous anti-Semitic forces were *induced* during the first few hours to start pogroms against the Jews, although it *proved very difficult* to persuade them."

This evidence of reluctance is completed by many instances of sympathy, help and positive support for which there is incontestable proof. Groups like the Quakers and Protestant as well as Catholic societies carried out widespread relief work. On the other hand, the number of those who risked making a public protest could, in the nature of things, only be small. Their voices were quickly silenced. Among those who had the courage to speak in unmistakable terms, the Dean of St. Hedwig's, Monsignore Bernhard Lichtenberg, may be mentioned. After the pogroms of November, 1938, he called upon the congregations of the Berlin cathedral to pray "for Jews and inmates of concentration camps". This and other demonstrations, such as his protest against the "mercy killing" of mental patients led to his arrest in October, 1942. While in prison he voluntarily applied for transfer to the ghetto in Lodz. He died on the way to Dachau in November, 1943. There was no lack of parallels on the Protestant side. And there were many cases of help by individuals and groups of which naturally no record was ever kept. Jews were maintained in hiding, helped to escape over the frontier or supplied with ration cards. Among those who took part in illegal work for the persecuted we may single out the Solf Group which centred round the widow and daughter of the former German foreign minister and ambassador in Tokio. They maintained close contacts with officials of the Diplomatic Service and, in particular, with the former German Consul General in New York, Otto C. Kiep, and with *Geheimrat* Kuenzer in the Foreign Office. Not least, the racial fanaticism of the régime brought people of humanitarian outlook together in opposition.

Further insight into the more systematic and conspiratorial activity of these humanitarian circles is afforded by Ruth Andreas-Friedrich's book, *Berlin Underground*. Her account of the resistance group "Uncle Emil" is written in diary form and though certainly not free of fictional traits bears the unmistakable stamp of truth. There was no political goal on which all members of this circle were agreed. Their common point of departure was a passionate abhorrence of the Hitler tyranny which they sought to oppose by all, including defeatist means, but above all, a basic determination to "serve the cause of humaneness" and to relieve as far as they could the tribulations of the oppressed. It will appear repeatedly in the course of this study that for many persons the mainspring of their opposition and its more generalised scope rested upon ethical and religious convictions or upon the irrepressible demands of simple human decency. "What we are doing," wrote Frau Andreas in her diary, "is individual work." But she adds the justifiable reminder : "When the day of reckoning comes, the fact that this individual work is being done by thousands upon thousands of Germans in the cause of humanity despite affliction, persecution and tyranny should not be forgotten by those who find it easier than we to be good and helpful human beings."

Such groups must have existed in other towns as well; examples are known in Munich and Augsburg. And in Berlin, "Uncle Emil" was certainly no isolated phenomenon. In 1947, the competent authority for Jewish affairs in the Berlin City Council stated that the majority of "Aryans" had never accepted Nazi anti-Semitism and that in the Reich capital alone, 5,000 Jews had successfully been hidden by their compatriots. This is certainly a pathetically small number compared with those who died. But the number of Germans who risked their lives to achieve even this comparatively small result must have been many times greater—and they should not be forgotten.

4. Intellectuals and Churches

The discussion of a silent Opposition merging by degrees into open non-conformism or very definite forms of underground activity leads to the central problem which particularly confronted intellectuals and the Churches. One might say that it was specifically their lot to sustain human inviolability and spiritual resistance. The question is, how far did they do justice to this task ?

In reply to this, no group has been more severely blamed than that of professors, journalists, writers and artists. And if it is true that they represent to a certain degree the conscience of a people then no criterion can indeed be strict enough. Here, as in the case of the Civil Service, it has been asserted that a widespread or, as as some people demand, a "unanimous" protest by German intellectuals would have hopelessly compromised the National Socialist régime and perhaps even brought about its collapse before it had time to consolidate its position. Something may be said for

C

this view although it calls to mind very obsolete forms of a political professorial class or of a revolutionary intelligentsia and in so far appears to be more "anachronistic" than the plans and actions of the German Opposition in fact were. None the less, it is true that no revolt of intellectuals took place in 1933 and that instances of weakness and disintegration multiplied. Only with a feeling of shame can one recall the invention of "German" mathematics or the many other forms of intellectual prostitution.

And the numerous defections of writers and men of learning were miserable indeed. It is also undoubtedly true that many tendencies in German academic life not only prepared the way for an excessive nationalism, but also contributed to that "anarchy of values" which created an all too fruitful soil for the brutality of the National Socialist dictatorship and the insipidity of Rosenberg's "Mythus". The number of old Nazis in the universities was indeed quite extraordinarily small and in almost every one of these isolated cases motives of professional rancour or personal inadequacy could be proved. But the co-ordination of academic life took place at a shameful speed and often anticipated with unnecessary compliance the show of force which, in the last resort, would certainly not have been lacking.

All this must be stated with an emphasis befitting the seriousness of the subject. It falls under the heading of the "Betrayal of the Intellectuals" or forms part of that broader phenomenon which a French writer has called the *trahison des clercs*. But the charge is one-sided. In order to balance it and for the sake of justice it would be necessary to mention also those who did not submit. There were leading men in philosophy and education, in history and jurisprudence, in philological studies, in economics and physics, and there were younger men among their colleagues who preserved themselves intact. But that alone would not be sufficient. It must further be remembered that on average a quarter of the students did not join the National Socialist Students' League, although to refrain might have made it impossible for them to remain at the university and endangered their future career. Further facts can be cited which create a more positive picture and probably had a more general significance. It is well known that a number of periodicals in no way surrendered their individual approach to affairs or their editorial independence: *Hochland,* for instance, and *Die Weissen Blätter,* or *Corona* and the *Deutsche Rundschau.* Similarly, a considerable number of

writers, poets and other artists refused to toe the line or were
actually involved in open opposition. One cannot suppose that
any of these attitudes did noticeable damage to the régime; their
effect was rather to give moral support to those engaged in active
resistance.

But in retrospect, particularly over the years of strongest pressure, there are further indications of the indestructibility of intellectual life and its purifying force. This can be seen both in the
intensity of intellectual effort in small circles and private gatherings and in the attitude of the reading public in general, in
theatre programmes and in the general tendencies of literary production. On 18th April, 1942, the *Frankfurter Zeitung* discussed
what it cautiously called "a certain reaction", that is, the preference of readers for "old books" and "works of greater profun-
dity". The same tendency is illustrated by the case of a bookseller
in a small town in Württemberg who made his shop the centre of
a lively exchange between authors and readers. Admittedly,
official Party publications were prominently displayed in the windows of publishers and booksellers, but this was to be expected
and the real business found other paths, offering goods to the
purchaser, if need be, under the counter, which did not bear the
stamp of arid uniformity and State-decreed tedium. Theological
treatises and the classics were much in demand, as well as trans-
lations of foreign literature. Popular editions of classical authors
appeared, among them a two-language edition of pre-Socratic
writers. Popular texts included Chinese philosophers as well as
Dante and Thomas Aquinas.

Scholarly literature, too, continued to be published with
astounding regularity. Frequently it was free of all Nazi colouring
and occasionally it was able to make a legitimate contribution to
the discouragement of legends. This even applied to historiography which was naturally under the strongest pressure. Critical
examination of specialised journals leads to the conclusion that
the number of contributions untainted by official catch-words was
greater than would be imagined. It was possible, for instance, to
publish an article proving that the "grave of Henry I" declared
by Himmler to be a national shrine belonged in fact to a Christian
female saint: whereupon the SS guards of honour were with-
drawn. And on the "German Historians' Day" in 1937, a leading
expert on the Middle Ages declared in very unorthodox fashion
that the development of the "Germanic" from the "Teutonic"

was due to the influence of antiquity and Christianity. In fact, it is not correct that the field of writing narrowed so extraordinarily. In 1946, the University of Bonn brought out a list of scientific publications dating from the years 1939 to 1945. It is clear that all National Socialist books, those adhering to the Party spirit and all other works conceivably on the Allied "Index" had been omitted. Nevertheless, the catalogue contains about 3,000 titles, principally in the field of cultural sciences. It is true that many of them indicate escapism to distant fields or at least a choice of subject remote from the danger zone. But the themes selected for emphasis are no less striking than the breadth of interest in general. Firstly, the viewpoint takes in Europe as a whole. In so far as it is concerned with German culture, it goes back emphatically to the older traditions: the Bible, Plato and Aristotle, Meister Eckhart, Nicholas of Cusa and Jakob Böhme, Humboldt and Schleiermacher, Goethe and Stifter. A German professor teaching in Switzerland, W. Röpke, who in general is strongly critical of his colleagues across the border, has well said that the insistence on intellectual continuity already represents a kind of opposition, although only in a passive form. But he also speaks of the transition leading from there to the forces of active resistance and adds : "We all have cause to do profound obeisance to the moral courage which was shown in this sphere."

In fact, the refusal to conform merges with more or less covert forms of resistance. From abstention it is only a step to an attitude which deliberately undermines National Socialist dogmas or which incites to opposition against a tyrannical régime in all its forms and effects. Even apparently conformist newspapers like the *Frankfurter Zeitung* could make use of certain weapons of attack, for instance their commercial columns. And if no other means were available, there always remained the sanctimonious publication of semi-official utterances, such as that the Japanese were "yellow Aryans" or that tomatoes were the "Nordic" fruit of the South.

Individuals could go further. In 1935, Adam von Trott zu Solz, a former Rhodes scholar who was to become one of the leading men in the conspiracy against Hitler, published the works of Heinrich von Kleist accompanied by a commentary. The relevance of the poet's attacks on Napoleon's tyranny to contemporary events was obvious. And Trott's introduction established beyond possibility of misunderstanding that Kleist became a rebel because he saw the "divine destiny" of man trodden in the dust and that he set his hopes on the "sense of uprightness of the individual citizen" who would rise against an immoral and demoralising despotism.

There were many examples of this indirect method of "laying aim", as the artilleryman would call it. One could hit the target by joining Demosthenes against Philip of Macedonia, or Burckhardt against Napoleon. The attack could take the form of a book on Cromwell or Robespierre, on Pilsudski or the mass hysteria of the Münster Anabaptists in the sixteenth century. The same technique of camouflage was successfully used by the *Deutsche Rundschau* in articles intended for a wider public and in fact circulated in hectographed copies. These were on subjects like Siberia or the South American dictator Lopez. With all candour the same newspaper declared in April, 1941, that megalomania was "one of the most dangerous diseases of a people".

As the eyes and ears of the Gestapo and the Propaganda Ministry were said to be ubiquitous, it may be asked how it was possible to carry out indirect attacks of this kind and preserve some sort of independence. The answer is that the very multiplicity of controlling bodies and the competition between them afforded some opportunity of evasion. In a particular case, that of Ernst Jünger's *Marmorklippen*, it has been suggested that Goebbels himself secretly enjoyed the book because its main attack seemed to be directed against the equivocal figure of a "Chief Forester" (Goering). In any case, Goebbels was clever enough to have no illusions about the deadly dullness of official Party literature and the Party press. To the theatre at least he accorded some freedom. In addition, writers and teachers possessed those safety-valves and bolt-holes already mentioned.

But all this had very definite limits. Rudolf Pechel, the editor of the *Deutsche Rundschau* and a member of the active Resistance movement from the beginning, was arrested in April, 1942, when one of his articles had the misfortune to be broadcast to Germany by the B.B.C. He and his wife and friends were interrogated by the usual methods and in the three years which he had to spend in a remand prison and in concentration camps he narrowly escaped death.

The case of Ernst Wiechert must also be remembered. In an "address to German youth" which he delivered at Munich University in 1935 he appealed to his audience ". . . not to keep silent

when conscience bids you speak because nothing in the world so
eats away the marrow of a man as cowardice". Wiechert himself
had finally to pay for his uncompromising attitude in Buchenwald. Other intellectuals and university teachers who joined the
active Opposition will be referred to later. At all events, a picture
painted only in black would be very unjust. Neither is it in any
way true that the opposition of intellectuals was confined to an
exclusive circle of "reactionary" or "liberalistic" thinkers and
could only be understood by initiates. It would be more appropriate to speak of a movement of "reaction" in the best sense of
the word, that is, of a turning back to eternal values, of a tapping
or revitalisation of energies which gave the political opposition a
broader and more fundamental basis.

The same applies to the Churches and indeed more to them
than to any other group of the Opposition. Here, too, it was not
easy to overcome hesitation and the tendency to compromise.
The unbridgeable contradiction in principle was not clear from
the very start. Only sects like the Quakers and the Mennonites
or the *Ernste Bibelforscher* remained free of hesitation. They
offered continual passive resistance, but their numbers were small.
As for the Catholic Church, the Vatican at first tried by the
conclusion of a Concordat (20th July, 1933) to continue a policy
which had not been successful in the Weimar period and at the
same time to raise bulwarks against the claims of the totalitarian
system and the spread of the new paganism. In these negotiations
Hitler was concerned to eliminate as far as possible any opposition
on the part of the German clergy and to gain the valuable propaganda point of refuting his own hostility to the Church. After
the Concordat had been signed, Vice-Chancellor von Papen tele-
graphed effusively from Rome : "Thanks to your broad, wise and
statesmanlike conception of the important task of the Christian
Churches in the construction of the Third Reich a work has now
been completed which will later be recognised as an historic deed
of National Socialism." In practice, as the further imposition of
uniformity and interference in the education of youth and Catholic social work soon showed, this "advance of confidence" on the
part of the Vatican proved ineffective. Moreover the political
significance of the Concordat was that the highest Church authority initiated the series of international treaties which helped to
legitimise the National Socialist régime and made it, as it were,
respectable.

As far as German Protestantism is concerned, its resistance was impeded by the tradition of a positive relationship between Church and State and the traditional conception of "Christian authority", as well as by certain characteristics of its social composition. In addition, the predominantly Lutheran part of German Protestantism looked to a doctrine which laid more stress on the supernatural than the visible world and was more interested in the cure of souls than in the Christian structure of social life. And indeed for Luther the outward order of things, which in any case belonged to the realm of sin, was of comparatively small importance. It could not be "reformed" by human endeavour, but only through faith and Christian charity. The rudiments of a right to resist founded on religion were not lacking in Luther, but they had become obscured by the historical development of German Protestantism. In the traditional interpretation, Luther's doctrine of the "two Kingdoms" differed from Calvin's in its purely transcendental orientation. All this comprised traditions and attitudes which were close to conservatism in the political and social sense, were an obstacle on the path to civil disobedience and still more to direct action and stressed the Bible commandment: "Render unto Caesar the things that are Caesar's."

But the National Socialist attack on both Churches and on Christianity in any form soon fanned the smouldering conflict into open flame. The history of the Battle of the Churches in the Third Reich has been so often told—abroad, too, it is the best-known part of the history of the Opposition—that only some basic characteristics need be mentioned here. Beside inflated or artificially fabricated charges raised against individual Catholic priests or Orders, beside the penetration attempted by the National Socialist shock troops of the "German Christians" into the Protestant Churches and Church administration, there broke out the basic conflict of principles of which the Cross and the swastika were the symbols. Thus the Catholic bishops and the Confessing Church did not merely raise their voices against Gestapo interference or attempts to disrupt the Churches from within. What they attacked was rather the National Socialist system itself in its essential characteristics: the totalitarian claim with its complete disregard for the sanctity of human life and its mockery of the most elementary conceptions of law; the reinterpretation of the Christian Faith on the basis of racial dogma; the deification of Hitler and the exaltation of the blood-community of the chosen German people.

Once this essential conflict had become clear there was no possibility of evading it. And it was not evaded. Anyone who reads Cardinal Faulhaber's sermons on the Old Testament·or the pastoral letters of the German bishops from as early as the summer of 1933, the "Declaration of Barmen" of May, 1934, or the official pronouncements of the Confessing Church will no longer be prepared to accept that "cowardly submissiveness" was the rule. The tone sharpened in keeping with events: in March, 1935, a manifesto against "racial mysticism" was read from Protestant pulpits. As a result, 700 clergy were arrested. The memorandum drafted at Whitsun, 1936, by the leaders of the Confessing Church and intended for Hitler himself went still further. It stated: "When blood, race, nationality and honour receive the status of eternal values, the Evangelical Christian is obliged by the first Commandment to reject this scale of values. When the Aryan man is exalted, God's word testifies to the sinfulness of all men. When in the framework of National Socialist ideology anti-Semitism is imposed on the Christian obliging him to hate the Jews, for him the Christian Commandment of brotherly love remains binding." Turning to the same basically human approach, a pastoral letter of the German bishops of 1942 stated: "We would stress particularly that we espouse not only religious and Church rights, but human rights as such. . . . Without their guarantee the whole structure of Western civilisation must collapse."

All this was not only preached. It was lived and endorsed by hundreds of pastors and church officials who were removed from their pulpits and their functions or put in prisons and concentration camps. According to American sources, upwards of 800 Catholic priests and 300 to 400 Evangelical clergy died in Dachau. While among the Catholic priests those from non-German countries, for instance Poland, probably predominated, the Evangelical pastors must in the main have been Germans.

This is the general picture of a spiritual resistance which it can be presumed will be generally agreed. But within this frame certain individual questions require critical discussion. And firstly, how far did the opposition of the Churches extend? In the two Confessions and in all ecclesiastical camps there were certainly differences of tactical procedure. Depending on the situation, there were differences between, on the one hand, the so-called "undestroyed" Protestant churches in South and West Germany and also in Hanover which were less endangered in the constitutional question and, on the other, the old Prussian church, the Union, which indeed stood with its back to the wall. Unanimity cannot be said to have existed, particularly in the Protestant ranks. Even in Berlin, which with Dahlem was the unofficial headquarters of the Confessing Church, there were in 1937 only 160 clergy who belonged to the C.C.; another forty were "German Christians" and 200 held a middle position. These figures certainly cannot be applied in a schematic fashion to party groupings among the clergy and—with the broad middle group —they indicate less a cleavage in the human than in the theological attitude. And here we touch a problem of considerable importance.

In many respects, National Socialism can be considered as the final summit and an extreme consequence of the secularisation movement of the nineteenth century. It follows that "liberal" Protestantism, which was imbued with an idealistic cultural philosophy and a metaphysic of progress, tended more to an attitude of *laisser faire* in outward things and possessed less power of resistance to Nazism. It must be clearly understood that the "radical" opponents of the régime were in the orthodox camp, that is to say, in the camp of those who adhered to an undiluted doctrinal position and to a pessimistic conception of the so-called natural or "demonic" forces in the world. While the Resistance movement was undoubtedly led by the orthodox section of the clergy and by the "Council of Brethren", it may well be wondered whether and to what extent the dogmatic approach was understood by the many who flocked to the churches. But even among the lay element an interest in theology became extraordinarily widespread.

Another question arising is whether the energetic attachment to religious opposition was not merely another form of escapism and helped actually to retard political resistance. Martin Niemöller, the most frequently mentioned of the leaders of the Confessing Church, has openly admitted the justification of this reproach, at least to the extent that the Evangelical Church only awoke to a realisation of the general danger after it had been attacked in its most intimate and inward concerns. When Protestant representatives of Germany met together with those of West European countries and the United States in the autumn of 1945 in Stuttgart, they declared themselves guilty of having neglected to offer earlier and more effective resistance to National Socialism. They accepted on behalf of the Church a share of the "war guilt" in the sense that no timely attempt had been made to bring about the fall of the Government.

Such a statement has, like every other expression of critical self-examination, an intrinsic value which should not be obscured by the imputation of tactical motives. Pharisaical hypocrisy would have been in flagrant contradiction to the impulses which became evident in the opposition of the Churches. But whether these impulses of self-criticism could, or in an earlier stage, should have led to direct political action is quite another question. It was clearly in the nature of things and a fact not to be regretted that spiritual protest and the defence of the Gospel came first. Only thus could a firmness of attitude grounded in suffering for the cause of the Christian Faith be achieved. Only so could passive resistance develop, though slowly, into a frontal attack on the essence of National Socialism, thereby becoming a total opposition to every totalitarian secular claim, not only to isolated encroachments on the part of the Government, but to its claim to control life in all its aspects. From the point of view of historical assessment, it is appropriate to ask whether, by defending themselves within their most intimate sphere, the Churches did not provide the forces of active resistance with a harder core and a sharper cutting edge than any outward revolt could have done.

This leads to a final question which concerns the degree of effectiveness of the Churches' opposition. More than once they undoubtedly deterred the Government from extreme measures. It is, for instance, known that the *Gauleiter* of East Prussia was obliged to warn the Party leadership against a policy which would have driven the peasants of the province, who were German and Masurian Protestants, into open rebellion. The appointment of the "Reich Bishop" Müller was a fiasco. A kind of popular rising in the county of Münster in 1936 secured the re-erection of the crucifix in school buildings. There was more than one such reverse for the Party and it can indeed be said that the Church opposition was the only one to achieve visible successes. Nevertheless, the number of persecuted individuals increased until after the outbreak of war the "cold" method of getting clergy out of the way by calling them up for service at the front became widely employed. But all too drastic clashes had to be avoided. Thus restraint was exercised in the case of the Bishop of Münster and neither the Government nor the Party intervened when Count von Galen delivered his famous "three sermons" in 1941 or in the following year when he attacked the criminal methods of the régime in occupied countries and the "mercy killings".

Still more important, however, was the effect of opposition on the Churches themselves. They gained unmistakably in inner vitality. Although questions of dogma were taken more seriously than in previous decades, the dividing lines between the Confessions lost in importance. Liturgical movements tending to the Una Sancta made their influence felt and a common front became apparent. Thus the Bishop of Berlin, Count Preysing, declared in 1937: "Never before have we been so deeply bound in love and common suffering with our brethren who diverge from us in the Faith." This Christian solidarity was a distinctive feature in the German Opposition. It found its expression in many cases of mutual support or joint action. In addition, for the first time since the middle of the nineteenth century the Church recovered lost ground. Not only did Communist and Christian prisoners learn to respect one another for the sincerity of their views and their will to make sacrifices, as Pechel and Wiechert have testified and many experienced, but apparently the courage shown by clergy and churchmen proved a recruiting element in Marxist circles which had long been estranged from Christianity. Impressive evidence of this can be found in the co-operation between leading groups of the conspiracy or in the Christian socialism of the Kreisau circle. Certainly, the crowds which thronged to the services in the Dahlem churches despite being spied upon were not impelled solely by religious motives. They were clearly seeking an expression of opposition in the only form available to them. But they could not fail to be moved by the intensity of faith which they encountered there. At times, when a manifesto was read out or the Gestapo intervened to confiscate the collections made for the persecuted, the congregations would start of their own accord to sing Luther's hymn: "A mighty fortress is our God." The old hymn became an expression of political as well as of religious protest.

But yet another aspect of the Battle of the Churches must be emphasised. For the very reason that the opposition here in question sprang from a religious foundation the front was directed against oppression in all its forms. It was therefore not decisive whether the attack on human dignity bore the National Socialist or some other stamp. The totalitarian principle was (like peace) indivisible and red concentration camps were no better than brown or black. This attitude led to certain difficulties when American officials first contacted men of the German Churches after the end of the war. Was the opposition to the Soviet system which they encountered not an echo of Goebbels' propaganda or a relic of nationalist and reactionary strivings or a clumsy speculation on disunity between the former Allies? One can assume that a better understanding of the motives and the inner necessity of this attitude has meanwhile prevailed. At any rate, it must be realised that a genuine Church opposition was only possible on the basis of principles which had nothing to do with opportunism and which therefore maintained the same anti-totalitarian front even after the fall of the Nazis. Pastor Bonhoeffer once said : "If we claim to be Christians, we must allow no room for tactical considerations."

Only on such a basis could an uncompromising attitude be preached and the protest of the Churches be developed into underground work and active political resistance. It was not easy for the Confessing Church to build up, for the purpose of training its clergy, a secret organisation which had to employ all the devices of political conspiracy. Such methods no doubt weighed on sensitive consciences. It was still more difficult for Christians of the twentieth century to fall back, as it were, on theories developed by Calvinists and Jesuits more than three centuries before which called on the "pious" to encompass the fall or even to destroy "godless" governments. That is not to say that the conflict was necessarily seen in such an historical perspective. In his penetrating essays written in prison, Bonhoeffer considered that Germans were only just beginning to discover the meaning of free responsibility. "It rests", he wrote, "on a God who demands the free witness to faith of responsible action and who promises forgiveness and comfort to him who becomes a sinner in the process." The best of the resistance knew that their actions lacked "ultimate justice" and remained subject to Grace. Here the inner gravity appears which the depth of such a conflict, once fought out, inevitably added to the political Opposition front. This front must now be considered.

PLANS AND ACTIONS

1. Early Centres of Resistance

IT is idle to inquire at what moment active political resistance to Hitler in fact began. In many of its initial forms it represented merely a continuation of the battles which had preceded the National Socialist seizure of power. The core of this early opposition was principally leftist and anti-Fascist circles. But conditions of "illegality" imposed new methods on them. The first party to be outlawed were the Communists. At a blow they saw themselves deprived of almost all their functionaries (nearly 4,000). But they had the advantage of a schooling in revolutionary technique and thus they created the pattern for the organisation of Resistance cells. A summary of their regulations issued for underground work has been preserved. A main requirement was that "members should in no circumstances have knowledge of the activity of any other cell but their own". Besides extensive measures for the purpose of security, the instructions laid great emphasis on sabotage in factories and on propaganda.

As for the parties of the Weimar coalition, the Social Democratic, the Democratic and the Centre Party, for a time they surrendered to the illusion that political opposition would be legally possible. There still seemed hope for the restoration of the rule of law and of parliamentary control. Had the elections of March, 1933, not clearly shown that, despite mass terror and the grossest intimidation, the non-National Socialist parties still held a majority? While the Communists with their dogmatic conceptions were convinced that Hitler was playing into their hands and merely hastening the collapse of bourgeois society, even the Socialists were at first inclined to look on the régime as a mere temporary setback compared with a normal democratic order. Thus the chairman of the Social Democrats, Otto Wels, declared at the last mass meeting of his party in Berlin : "Harsh rulers do not govern long." But these illusions were destroyed piecemeal by the Reichstag fire and the subsequent arrests, by the Enabling Law of 23rd March which in practice abolished the prerogatives

45

of the Reichstag and the Reich President and which only Wels dared to oppose in open debate, by the dissolution and expropriation of the trade unions and finally, in July, 1933, by the ban on all parties except the National Socialists. Thus illegality became the only possible course.

The question has often been asked why, from the very start, force was not answered with force or, if that did not seem possible, why resort was not had to a general strike, the weapon that thirteen years earlier had proved so successful in the suppression of the Kapp Putsch. Those who argue thus tend to overlook the confusing and paralysing effect of completely new experiences as well as the weight of the evolutionary and legalistic traditions to which the Social Democrats and the trade unions adhered. Moreover, the *coup d'état* of the National Socialists was not, in fact, a *Putsch*, in other words, an armed uprising; it was carried out in a pseudo-legal and -democratic fashion as a "step-by-step" revolution and it found support among wide sections of the population, particularly the unemployed and the *petite bourgeoisie*. Even disregarding this cleavage in the masses which would have made the success of a strike very improbable, the disunity of the German proletariat was a serious factor. More than once, despite frequent bloody clashes, the Communists and the National Socialists had joined hands as allies. It had happened in 1931 when they had jointly attacked the Social Democratic Government in Prussia and again a year later, when both parties had supported a wild-cat strike of Berlin transport workers. It is also beyond doubt that after January, 1933, many "Red Front" activists found their way into the SA, though hardly in so flagrant a fashion or in such numbers as has been suggested and as occurred in the reverse direction in the Soviet Zone after 1945. It is also clear that the phase of the Hitler-Stalin alliance (August, 1939 to June, 1941) brought the extremes considerably closer together even in internal politics. On instructions from Moscow many Communists crossed over at that time to the National Socialist side, as occurred also in a different fashion in France. Hence it must be realised that a potential "totalitarian" front ran across the "proletarian" front and that, for different reasons, both anti-democratic wings looked on the Social Democratic Party as the real "traitors" while the latter had less cause than ever to submit to Moscow.

These are facts which were to play a very considerable part in the history of the German Opposition. Socialists and Communists continued to go their separate ways. Not even in the period of the "Popular Front" policy (1936 to 1939) was a real understanding achieved between them. In 1934, the executive of the Social Democratic Party which had emigrated to Prague did indeed adopt a revolutionary programme advocating the class struggle. But it soon returned to reformism in its basic conceptions, particularly after it had been obliged to transfer its place of exile to Paris, London and Washington. And it emphatically declined to subordinate itself to the Third Internationale (even in a disguised form).

Now there were indeed many separate Socialist groups of a radical kind principally supported by the younger generation who wished to dissociate themselves from the pre-Hitler groupings and from obsolete Party principles. In the autumn of 1933, a brochure written in Germany but published in Carlsbad appeared under the title: "New Beginning, Fascism or Socialism". The author ("Miles") pleaded not only for unity in the proletarian front, but sought to give a realistic interpretation of the essence of the National Socialist dictatorship and draw practical conclusions from it. He disavowed the hope that a régime based on force would inevitably collapse from within and stressed the need for forming "élite cadres", a secret and firmly cohesive organisation of experienced individuals who would have theoretical and practical schooling and maintain contact with important groups of industrial employees. While this programme, which was built on the assumption of a coming large-scale international crisis, proved apposite in the long run, the "illegal" opponents of the régime were in the meantime passing through bitter experiences. In their turn, almost all the "New Beginners" were forced into exile. Leaders of the Democratic and Centre Parties, exposed to increasing persecution, were also forced sooner or later to leave their homeland. All as far as possible maintained contact with the remnants of their parties. But co-operation between the three main groups was often inhibited by mistrust. And the small measure of support which they found abroad was a heavy disappointment.

Despite these reverses, for a time secret activity sharply increased. Germany was flooded with illegal brochures and pamphlets smuggled in through the "frontier secretariats" or printed on secret presses. Every possible trick and strategem was used to camouflage the propaganda campaign and make the distribution anonymous. Whole pages could be filled with a description of these practices or with quotations from underground literature. Another field of activity was the smuggling out of reports from Germany. They supplied information on political, economic and military events or gave instances of resistance, planned delaying tactics by the workers or of the defeat of Nazi candidates for factory appointments. In their reports "from inside Germany" the political committee in exile also strove to disseminate everything calculated to encourage internal or external opposition.

But the Gestapo improved its technique and drew the net ever tighter. Infiltration succeeded, particularly into Communist groups. It was the working population which had to bear the brunt of the counter-attacks. Losses were heavy. In 1934, the *Manchester Guardian* wrote of the "ten thousand unknown heroes". In the following year a new wave of terror began. Observers with experience of underground party work agreed that under the prevailing conditions too much rather than too little was being attempted in Germany. They criticised the participation of large numbers of people who felt attracted by the romance of secret society work or whose thirst for adventure found satisfaction in battles with the police. Could mass propaganda seriously endanger the Nazi régime, or the theft and concealment of a handful of weapons lead to a change in the situation sufficiently drastic to justify the losses incurred? Did the practical moral effect of placards posted or catchwords painted on walls stand in any justifiable relationship to the risk? To provoke or mislead the Gestapo may well have had its attractions. But in the last resort these methods were suicidal. It seemed more important to save the Resistance cells in the workers' movement and in the Socialist and Christian trade unions. Old centres had to be preserved intact, new members carefully selected and methodically trained. The long-term effect of this reorientation should not be overlooked. It contributed to the formation of that "reserve front" of a silent Opposition, already mentioned, which could be counted upon. But, from 1935 onwards, the direct result of the change of tactics was a certain reduction in the scope of overt agitation.

Meanwhile, within the Nazi Party the severe crisis had developed which is known to history as the Röhm Putsch and which found an outlet in the blood-bath of 30th June, 1934, and the following days. The question arises whether there were not possibilities here for some early action on the part of the Resistance, whether they helped to shape the crisis and hence whether this crisis belongs to the object of our study. In a direct sense this is certainly not the case. Primarily, the events of June were concerned with the suppression of malcontents and of tendencies to a "second revolution" within the Party, secondarily, with a struggle for power between the Army and the SA from which the SS emerged the actual winners. Indirectly, however, the massacre definitely had something to do with the history of the active Resistance movement. It afforded final clarity about the character of the régime. Though it was not known at the time that the number of victims amounted to two or three times the officially admitted figure of "only" seventy-seven, the cynical brutality of the ruling clique and the declaration of murder as a legal instrument opened the eyes of many people. Moreover, the extent of the blood-bath raises the question whether merely old scores were settled or whether opponents outside the Party had at least a part in the crisis.

A symptom in this direction was the unusually polemical tone of a speech delivered by Vice-Chancellor von Papen on 17th June, 1934, to the students at Marburg University. It can be taken as inspired if not actually written by the Munich lawyer, Edgar J. Jung. How far Papen himself was prepared to draw conclusions from the reproaches raised in the speech remains an open question. Though professing regard for Jung in his memoirs, he places him at a distance and suggests he would still be alive if he had not declared himself to be "the soul of the Papen resistance". The genuineness of Jung's opposition and his relation to the June crisis is not, however, open to doubt. He belonged to a group of "Young Conservatives" comprising resolute Christians of both Confessions. Like other supporters of the Right, they had long since broken with the nationalistic and materialistic views of Hugenberg's pseudo-Conservatism. But they also recognised the dangers associated with certain offshoots of pseudo-Liberalism, namely with the lack of cohesion of an atomised and de-Christianised society or a secularised mass civilisation which was liable to capsize into demagogy and dictatorship. Most of them sympathised with federalistic principles and with a European order based on national autonomy (not on centralised sovereign states) and on co-operative organisations after the pattern of the trade unions. In Munich Jung himself had been able to observe the rise and character of the National Socialist movement at close

D

quarters and had attracted attention in the Weimar period with a book bearing the provocative title, *The Rule of the Inferiors* (1928–30). That he reacted even more strongly to Hitler as the Anti-Christ is beyond question. He may, as others did, have hoped to find the fulcrum for action in a Vice-Chancellor disillusioned by events, particularly when the conflict brewing in the Party had burst into the open. Pechel, who belonged to the same circle, asserts that Jung and his friends had definite plans for overthrowing the Government and that the Marburg speech was intended as a signal. However that may be, there were undoubtedly contacts with Treviranus who in the early thirties had built up an anti-Hugenberg and anti-Nazi front of the moderate Right and with Dr. Brüning, the leader of the Centre Party and the last democratic Chancellor of the Weimar Republic. It seems that both men were intended to play an active part in the crisis—both escaped the blood-bath by a narrow margin. On the other hand, others outside the Party who fell victim to it were probably known and hated as opponents and they were liquidated because instinct suggested them as possible focal points of opposition, although they did not seem to be involved in actions or plans. This applies to Papen's secretary, von Bose, and to the head of his ministerial bureau, the leader of "Catholic Action", Erich Klausener. And it probably also applies to Generals von Schleicher and von Bredow. Conspiratorial relations on their part with Röhm or with France certainly did not exist.

Whatever other factors may have been at work in the background during these days, in the criss-cross of relationships between various social strata and across all party barriers the impression is confirmed that the character of the Opposition changed and began to consist more of individual personalities or groups which combined spontaneously on the basis of motives which may often have had their common denominator in moral indignation or in sympathy with every form of rebellion, whatever its specific starting point. A striking example of this is the typical non-conformist and nationalist revolutionary, Ernst Niekisch. Schlabrendorff relates that at the beginning of 1933 he and some of his Conservative friends liberated Niekisch from an SA cellar where he and other Nazi opponents were held prisoner. During the blood-bath of 30th June, Niekisch in turn concealed a close associate of the Schlabrendorff circle, Ewald von Kleist, a descendant of an old Prussian Junker family. The connections here made are of great symptomatic interest. Niekisch was known as the head of a publishing house and publisher of a periodical, both of which bore the name "Resistance". Originally, his nationalist revolutionary front was directed as much against Weimar as against the National Socialist and Communist Parties. And when in 1932 he published an article under the title, *Hitler—a German Disaster*, he attacked the future dictator because, amongst other reasons, he was too "western" in thought and was therefore destroying the genuine revolution. At the same time something of the Prussian spirit was alive in Niekisch and it made him declare: "Hitler, the Austrian, is the revenge for König-grätz." Niekisch continued the polemic in brochures of extreme asperity not, as it seems, without the support of Army circles. That a man of this kind could work together with the Young Conservative opposition certainly indicates some unusual cross-connections. In 1937, Niekisch was arrested for plotting high treason and condemned to life-long imprisonment.

There were many other groups of men and women in opposition who were loosely organised on a local basis or round an individual personality. One of them, centred on a swashbuckler from the volunteer corps Oberland by name "Beppo" Roemer, agreed at an early stage on the necessity of killing Hitler. The circle received regular information about the *Führer's* daily programme from contacts in the Berlin military headquarters and the Foreign Office. But plans were never put into effect. An idealist like Nikolaus von Halem, who had already reached the conclusion after 30th June, 1934, that only force would avail against the "messenger of chaos", seems also to have been involved in Roemer's attempts and, together with *Legationsrat* Mumm von Schwarzenstein, was hurled to destruction by their discovery. While awaiting death he wrote to a friend of that profound experience when "the self starts to become so shadowy", and to his mother a few minutes before his execution: "Now I have overcome that last slight trepidation that seizes the tree-top before it falls."

The "Avengers of Röhm", known as the "R.R.s", were probably of a very different type. There were also individuals and outsiders who went their own ways. But the cabinet-maker G. Elser who made the attempt on Hitler's life in the Bürgerbräu cellar in Munich on 8th November, 1939, can hardly be reckoned among the solitary fanatics. Although the attempt has been made to include him in the history of the Resistance as a Communist master-assassin acting on his own initiative, there can be no doubt that the installation of a time bomb would have been impossible without the assistance of the Gestapo and that, as planned, Hitler's speech was broken off before the explosion. The incident actually prejudiced the work of the Opposition in that it strengthened Hitler's consciousness of his "mission" and it seemed to open the series of "providential" escapes. Moreover, as will be shown later, it acted as a disturbing factor in an attempt that was really planned. Besides, Himmler used the incident as a pretext to demand the arrest of forty Bavarian legitimist "accomplices" and officially the British Secret Service was accused of the plot. This is the only bomb incident to be made public from the pre-war period, but it can be assumed that other attempts were made which were not so generally known. Even the American corres-pondent William L. Shirer, who certainly paid no particular attention to symptoms of resistance in his neighbourhood, reports in his *Berlin Diary* two such explosions in a single night.

But in the framework of this study it seems more important to stress that even among the early centres of resistance many of the names already appear which point forward to the history of 20th July, 1944. The composition of these groups illustrates the spread of an oppositional spirit growing out of basically new experiences under the Nazi régime. Thus, during these years, individuals and groups sowed seeds not with a view to immediate action but in preparation for action. Pechel, who had manifold contacts, cites among other well-known personalities : the Communists Saefkow, Jakob and Bästlein; the Socialists Ernst von Harnack (the son of the theologian), Doctors Mischler and Markwitz; the Centrists Andreas Hermes and Jakob Kaiser. He mentions particularly men like Schulze-Boysen and Arvid Harnack whom we have already met as leaders of the "Red Chapel". He further mentions industrialists like von Halem and Reusch or the circle round Robert Bosch in Stuttgart which, amongst other oppositional activities, financed the *Deutsche Rundschau*. Pechel's list also in-cludes artists, professors, lawyers, doctors and individuals from all walks of life.

Of particular interest at this stage of development is an obser-vation which Schlabrendorff made in the year 1938. After work-ing for some time as a lawyer in the provinces (Rhein-Hessen and Pomerania) on the formation of anti-Nazi cells, he found on his return to Berlin a "changed picture". Whereas the Opposition had previously consisted of a loose mosaic of the forces which had been in the lead before 1933, there was now, though still no "firm organisation", an interplay in which these forces were developing. "There were numerous circles in existence which were mutually intersecting." The bond which held so many disparate elements together was apparently more their common ethical convictions than social interests. Into this changed picture fitted the founding of the "German Freedom Party" in the years 1937–38. Their first pamphlet stressed "the dignity of the human personality" as the rallying point of all opponents of the Nazi régime. It also underlined the fact that the political aim should not be a mere return to Weimar. That was a demand for a radical readjustment which could count on wide support.

The question arises whether there were other and more solid nuclei besides the underground cells of the workers and the parties of the Left, besides the loose and newly forming groups of people whose conscience had been aroused. Were there, in particular, such active centres within the key positions of the State which had so far been only partially imbued with the Nazi spirit or not at all, that is, in the Foreign Office, in civil administration and in the Army?

The problem of "toeing the line" which was of particular urgency for higher officials has already been touched on. In a penetrating study on authority and resistance (*On the Political Sociology of Officialdom*) Herbert von Borch has come to the conclusion that opposition under a dictatorship "had the best prospects of success in the very earliest stages and that it can only be effective, if at all, within the ruling civil or military apparatus". That leads to the question of the institutionalisation of the law and of a civil servant's duty to resist which is not for discussion here. The problem as such was certainly not a conscious one in 1933, though it had a certain precedent in the "resistance of the High Officialdom" during the Kapp Putsch. But as we have already emphasised, the Nazi seizure of power was not a Putsch. Any kind of front against pseudo-legality was unthinkable in the higher Civil Service and only in the efforts of individuals can one speak of an early Opposition in these key spheres of gövernment.

In the Foreign Office a number of individuals can be included in the early Opposition over the years though precise dates are not available in every case. Besides those already mentioned or

reserved for special discussion later, the following may be cited :
Dr. Robert A. Ulrich, E. von Salzam, Dr. Siegfried, von der
Heyden-Rynsch, Dr. Georg von Bruns, Dr. Ad. Velhagen,
Herbert Blankenhorn, Eduard Brücklmeier, Gottfried von Nostiz,
Dr. von Twardowski and Dr. Aschmann. In addition to resistance
work within their profession, information was passed to oppositional circles. In this respect, Dr. Paul Schmidt was a not unimportant figure since he took part as interpreter in all Hitler's
international conferences. It is certain that many members of the
Foreign Office—like other civil servants—took exception at the
very least to the corruption and arbitrariness which they encountered everywhere in the fulfilment of their duties. They were
conscious of serving the nation and not a particular form of
government, let alone a *Weltanschauung* and the system deduced
from it. It is also true that Bernhard Wilhelm von Bülow, Secretary of State in the early years of the régime, successfully
thwarted attempts at National Socialist infiltration and confined
concessions to the minimum. As late as the autumn of 1944,
Gauleiter Bohle complained to Himmler that among 690 high
officials in the Foreign Office more than 600 did not yet possess
"the right faith".

The foreign policy of the Nazi Government had therefore to
create its own organ, at first the foreign political office of the
National Socialist Party under Rosenberg, which achieved small
success, and then the Ribbentrop Bureau. When this was set up
in April, 1934, at first with the special task of "disarmament" but
with the clear intent of monopolising ever wider spheres, Dr.
Erich Kordt was attached as liaison officer. On his appointment
he was instructed to keep the Foreign Office continually informed
of Ribbentrop's activities and to prevent as far as possible his
interference in matters which did not concern him. Therewith
began war on a minor scale which technically certainly amounted
to opposition. But at first the watchword was to wait until the
régime, perhaps after some initial successes, should come to a
dead-end. In the long run, however, the result was the formation
of an important centre of resistance in Ribbentrop's closest entourage. The significance of this will be discussed later. Here suffice
it to say that Kordt was also in constant contact with Dr. Brüning.
Liaison between the Foreign Office and the Supreme Command
of the Armed Forces was also in anti-Nazi hands in the persons
of Kessel, a friend of Kiep, and von Etzdorf.

Even less than in the Foreign Office can one speak of the formation of an early and definite opposition front in the civil administration. But here, too, besides the phenomenon already mentioned of silent resistance or secret sabotage there were some outstanding individuals who started to resist in the initial stage. As an example the Secretary of State in the Prussian Ministry of the Interior, Herbert von Bismarck, may be mentioned. He protested against the illegality of the persecutions and resigned when he failed to persuade the non-Nazi ministers (in particular, von Blomberg) to take the same step. A further instance is that of *Landrat* Steltzer whose name we will meet again in connection with the Kreisau circle. In 1933, he circulated a memorandum in which he sharply criticised the régime in almost all its aspects and declared war on it from a religious standpoint. He was relieved of office and proceedings were started against him for high treason, but it never came to a trial. Another opponent in the administration, Carl Friedrich Goerdeler, will be referred to later. He became one of the central figures of the Resistance. But for a long time he, too, was and remained in office. Coming from local government where he became one of the leading municipal politicians in Germany, first as second Burgermaster in Königsberg and then as Oberburgermaster in Leipzig, then Price Commissar under Brüning, he later no doubt regretted not having accepted the offer of a ministry under Papen. From a deep sense of responsibility and in a belief habitual to him that good could always be achieved through reasonable persuasion, he accepted from Hitler in November, 1934, the post of Price Commissar and held it until July, 1935. His memorandum campaign continued, however, to be unsuccessful. There is no question that, before it ever came to a break and thereafter throughout the prewar years, Goerdeler worked for close co-operation between opponents of Nazism inside and outside Germany. He devoted himself to building an active opposition in his circle of acquaintances, principally among senior civil servants and business men. As Price Commissar he became increasingly opposed to Schacht's financial policy. Schacht himself, whose intellectual ability is as little in doubt as his gift for adapting himself to circumstances, went over to the Opposition at the latest in the year 1936 and in protest against the rearmament programme. Gisevius has given a dramatic (and probably overdramatised) account of a secret meeting which was planned but failed to take place between Schacht and the Commanding General in Münster, von Kluge, and which Gisevius claims to have arranged at the beginning of 1937. According to another source of information, late in 1936 Schacht sent a close friend to Colonel-General Beck with the inquiry whether he was prepared to proceed against Hitler. Beck is said to have replied that a change of régime was a matter for civilians, but that if the civil opposition took the initiative, the Army would not be found wanting. It was indeed a matter for civilians, that is, for citizens and the Opposition was to retain this character of an essentially civil resistance. And yet around 1937 all Resistance groups were agreed on one experience : under the Nazi system an unarmed movement held not the smallest prospect of success, either in a revolution after the barricade style, or a popular insurrection or in any other form of spontaneous rising, or in a revolution from above, whether started by a conspiracy within the régime or by leading men in society or officialdom. Whatever preparatory significance the early Resistance groups may have had, the next essential was to break the chains of the Gestapo and the SS. That could only be done by soldiers. And so people began to talk of the "Generals"—in a collective sense that had hitherto not been customary in Germany.

And here a number of problems arise which require special discussion.

2. Crisis in the Autumn of 1938

But before we discuss the military Resistance and again emphasise the basically civilian character of the Opposition we must consider the first attempt at combined action. This was quite distinct from all previous projects and derived its particular character from Hitler's war policy which was heading for catastrophe. In a conference on 5th November, 1937, of which a record was kept by Colonel Hossbach, Hitler revealed for the first time in the presence of the Foreign Minister, the War Minister and the Commanders-in-Chief of the three Services his resolve to settle the question of German "living-space" by force. Objections were raised by Neurath, Blomberg and Fritsch, but in the context were naturally confined to the diplomatic and technical military aspects. Colonel-General Beck, the Chief of the General Staff, reacted more sharply and there is evidence that he was deeply disturbed by Hossbach's record. Both as an expert confronted with dilettantish frivolity and as a key figure bearing moral responsibility, his objections to this catastrophic policy grew as Hitler's aggressive plans against Czechoslovakia developed until at the end of May, 1938, they became crystallised as an "irrevocable decision". Beck expounded his objections in three weighty memoranda addressed to von Brauchitsch, the Commander-in-Chief of the Army, and he reinforced them verbally. In one of the memoranda (of 16th July) occurs the passage since frequently quoted concerning the limits of soldierly obedience: "It reveals a lack of calibre and of understanding of his task when at such times a soldier in the highest position sees his duties and obligations only in the limited framework of his military tasks without realising the high responsibilities he bears towards the whole people. Extraordinary times call for extraordinary actions."

The spirit of resistance here expressed by Beck was not, however, to be confined to criticism from the expert's point of view or to the purely military obstruction which was at first planned by him in the form of a unanimous refusal by Army leaders to take part in Hitler's war project. Already the memorandum of 16th July contemplated "internal political tensions". On 29th July, Beck was more explicit: the Army must not only prepare for a possible war, but also "for an internal conflict which need only take place in Berlin". For this, he said, certain tasks should be allotted, and he mentioned von Witzelben, the commanding General in Berlin, and the Police President, Graf Helldorff.

This memorandum of 29th July, 1938, has rightly been considered the starting point for the planning of the *coup d'état* which was continued by Beck's successor, Halder. In particular, the Chief of the General Staff's advisers in the Information and Intelligence Service considered that if the German people were enlightened about the fateful trend which events were clearly taking the spell would be broken which the series of Hitler's successes in foreign policy—the achievement of freedom to re-arm, the occupation of the Rhineland and the *Anschluss* with Austria —had cast upon many people. If it could be shown beyond doubt that the régime was pursuing a war-mongering policy, then it would be easy to bring about the fall of the Government. The various groups of conspirators who had come together since 1937 were agreed on these conclusions. They not only resolved to do everything possible to prevent a European war; in the threat to peace they saw a uniquely favourable opportunity to secure wide support for a *coup d'état*.

There is no doubt that their analysis of public opinion was correct. This can be confirmed by anyone who had an oppor-tunity to observe the German people in the critical weeks prior to the Munich Agreement. It was not merely that the man in the street, indulging in wishful thinking and without knowledge of inside events, acclaimed the British Prime Minister, the peace-bringer "in our time", as enthusiastically as the British public. There were other, very striking occurrences. When on 27th Sep-tember Hitler paraded one of the new panzer divisions through Berlin—as a threatening gesture or to test or raise morale—the demonstration was watched in icy silence. Hitler himself experi-enced a similar response when he "showed himself to the people" on the balcony of the Reich Chancellery. The customary acclam-ation was lacking. At the peak of the international crisis there were clear signs of a severe crisis of confidence in the régime.

Whether this was fully foreseen by the conspirators remains an open question. At any rate, they counted on a reverse which would either force the dictator to give in and so lose face or else, if he continued on the road to catastrophe, make it possible to arraign him on a charge of war-mongering. Beside the individuals named by Beck and decisive for the control of power in Berlin (von Witzleben and Graf Helldorff) the Area Commandant of Potsdam, Graf Brockdorff-Ahlefeldt, had been won over to the conspiracy. In addition, a panzer division under General Hoepner stood ready in Thuringia to frustrate a possible attempt by the Munich SS Life-Guards to relieve Berlin. It would be rash to suggest that the plans were inadequate from the technical point of view or that insufficient forces were available to carry out the Putsch. The weakness of the plan lay rather in the assumption that the Western democracies would oppose Hitler's aggression against Czechoslovakia and thereby make the danger of a general war plain for all to see. But it must be added that everything possible was done to persuade at least Great Britain to act in this way.

This leads to the political side of the action. Goerdeler, who had not stinted his warnings in England in the summer of 1937, did not participate at this stage; from August to October he stayed in Switzerland. The initiative in the sphere of international politics was undertaken in August partly by the Intelligence and partly by the Resistance group in the Wilhelmstrasse and led to steps of a drastic nature such as the history of no other Resistance movement can show.

A prelude was the mission organised by the Intelligence of Ewald von Kleist-Schmenzin who on behalf of "his friends" went to London on 18th August and had discussions mainly with Vansittart and Churchill. He stated categorically that Hitler's war plan had been drawn up and would be put into effect after 27th September. The Generals opposing such a course meanwhile needed encouragement from outside. Kleist therefore urged a firm declaration by Britain and an appeal to the German Opposition. If war could be avoided, this would represent the prelude to the end of the régime. In discussion with Churchill he went further and stressed that if the Generals insisted on peace, a new government would be formed within forty-eight hours. While Vansittart informed the Prime Minister, Churchill wrote a letter to Kleist in which he predicted a general blood-bath if the Germans proceeded to the attack. The Prime Minister, Neville Chamberlain, gave none of the desired undertakings; his thoughts on the preservation of peace followed different paths. And while acknowledging the genuineness of Kleist's hostility to Nazism, he evidently recoiled from his readiness for "civil disobedience" though this had been a very glorious English tradition during the wars of religion : the whole reminded him, he wrote, of the Jacobites in France at the time of William III.

The next highly unusual step was taken at the approach of the critical period, i.e. of the Nuremberg Party Rally (5th September), by Secretary of State von Weizsäcker in agreement with Beck. A female cousin of Erich Kordt was sent with a message whose text she had learnt by heart to his brother Theo who was at that time Chargé d'Affaires in London. After contacting Chamberlain's closest adviser, Sir Horace Wilson, Theo Kordt asked to be received in secret at the Foreign Office. On the night of 7th September he was admitted to 10 Downing Street by the garden entrance and gave Lord Halifax a statement formulated by von Weizsäcker and expressly made in the name "of political and military circles in Berlin which desire by all means to prevent a war". The statement stressed the necessity of an unambiguous attitude on the part of the British Government to Hitler's warmongering. If his policy of force was given free rein "the way for a return to conceptions of decency and honour among European nations would be finally closed". It was possible, stated von

Weizsäcker, that a frank British statement would prevent war and the National Socialist régime could not survive such a diplomatic defeat. But if Hitler none the less persisted in his war policy, Kordt declared himself in a position to guarantee that the political and military circles for which he spoke "will take arms against a sea of troubles and by opposing end them".

While the quotation from Hamlet underlined the unusual and dramatic character of the message, Weizsäcker ended with a clear promise: "If the desired statement is made, then the leaders of the Army are ready to proceed against Hitler by force of arms." The British Foreign Secretary listened with the closest attention to these extremely frank revelations and replied that he would inform the Prime Minister and one or two colleagues, treating the matter as highly confidential.

In Berlin, meanwhile, a wide variety of plans were on foot in military circles. Naturally, a setback was experienced when Chamberlain decided to fly to Berchtesgaden. But in the critical days of Godesberg when Hitler's increased demands led to a standstill in negotiations there still seemed a possibility of striking a blow. Beck had meanwhile been dismissed (27th August), though the fact was not made public for a time. But his successor, General Halder, was ready to strike and orders for an action which was to begin on the morning of 29th September were prepared. It seems that Brauchitsch also was now won over to the conspiracy. Then, at midday on 28th September, the news came that Chamberlain and Daladier had accepted the invitation to meet at Munich. It has been stated that this sensational information ran "like an electric shock" through the circles concerned, and the result was that the whole basis of the plan collapsed.

A fortnight later, Goerdeler wrote to an American friend: "... The German people did not want war; the Army would have done anything to avoid it; ... the world had been warned and informed in good time. If the warning had been heeded and acted upon Germany would by now be free of its dictator and turning against Mussolini. Within a few weeks we could have begun to build lasting world peace on the basis of justice, reason and decency. A purified Germany with a government of decent people would have been ready to solve the Spanish problem without delay in company with Britain and France, to remove Mussolini and with the United States to create peace in the Far East. The way would have been open for sound co-operation in economic and social fields, for the creation of peaceful relations between Capital, Labour and the State, for the raising of ethical concepts and for a fresh attempt to raise the general standard of living ..."

These views may be thought too optimistic in the confidence they place on a basic reorientation and its scope. And it lies in the nature of things that nobody can say whether the first step, the Putsch, would have been successful. But it is beyond question that the prospects opened were extremely promising in a general sense and concerned more than purely military spheres. The action was not planned merely to avoid a war which on sober calculation Germany would have been bound to lose. Rather it was part of a general aim which sought to restore human decency in international as well as in internal affairs. It is this vision of an alliance beyond national frontiers between the friends of peace which lends the episode historical grandeur in the apparently irresistible stream of tragic events. With the marked sense of honesty which Indians had already praised in the former Viceroy, Lord Halifax—they called him "the tall Christian"— the British Foreign Secretary said to Theo Kordt a few days after Munich: "We were not able to be as frank with you as you were with us. At the time that you gave us your message we were already considering sending Chamberlain to Germany." The same fairness should be apllied to the assessment of the whole course of the crisis during which German generals and diplomats set aside the usual standards of professional duty in the interests of a higher cause. Their attitude certainly did not show the oft-conjured "subservience" to an abstract idea of the State and revealed anything but an attitude of blind obedience.

It would lead us too far to describe here the numerous isolated acts of oppositional diplomacy which took place before and after Munich. Parallel with Kordt's action, Weizsäcker sought to bring pressure to bear on London in the sense of a powerful and immediate diplomatic démarche through the High Commissioner of the League of Nations in Danzig, the Swiss historian Carl J. Burckhardt. Burckhardt considered the step so important that he travelled without a stop from Berlin to Berne to discharge his task with the British Minister there. More and more then the oppositional elements in the German Foreign Office pursued the aim of avoiding war by applying a brake as both the Italian Ambassador Attolico and von Weizsäcker had defined it. Such a policy stood in clear contradiction to Hitler's plans and Ribbentrop's instructions. It continued the line of 1938, that is, it sought firmness in London against extortions under the threat of force, but it also sought a peaceful solution of the contested issues between Germany and Poland. There is plenty of evidence that both lines were pursued. But this study is not so much concerned with the policy of maintaining peace as such—however much this belongs under the moral title of the German Opposition—as with its connection with direct revolt against the régime and with plans for its fall. Even after Munich these plans were not abandoned, though they did not attain the fateful and dramatic intensity of September, 1938. Halder himself was not a personality of Beck's calibre, and Hitler's success at Munich as well as his unopposed occupation of Prague in March, 1939, enhanced the prestige of the "sleep-walker". Moreover, it seemed questionable on the one hand whether the Western democracies would ever be prepared to resist Hitler's attacks by force of arms and, on the other, the German Foreign Office could not welcome the decision on war or peace falling into Polish hands as a result of the British defensive alliance with Poland.

While in these circumstances the Opposition undertook no action with a decisive aim, individual elements of the Resistance went very far in their efforts regarding Britain, to mention only the visits of Goerdeler, Pechel and Schlabrendorff to London and Trott's initiative. A particularly striking attempt to dislocate the official policy is again associated with the brothers Kordt. According to express confirmation by Lord Halifax, they kept the British Government continually informed of the darkening political horizon and gave timely warning of the impending agreement between Hitler and the Soviet Union—all this through Lord Vansittart whose memory proved so much at fault in this respect.

If a situation of balance, for which Weizsäcker still hoped as a means of preventing war, could not be achieved, it was still preferable for the West to come to an understanding with Moscow. For as Kordt formulated: "In the present situation we must prefer even the risk of temporary encirclement of National Socialist Germany to the certainty of a second world war which might mean the end of Western civilisation." Kordt and his friends were thus prepared to walk a tightrope and seek the diplomatic defeat of Germany for the sake of preserving peace.

From these details, which represent an epilogue to the action planned with "the Generals" in the autumn crisis of 1938, we turn to a more basic discussion of the role played by the military sector under the Nazi dictatorship and within the framework of the Resistance movement.

3. Military Sector

The relationship between the Army and the Party forms one of the main problems in the history of the Third Reich. It cannot be covered by a simple formula. We can dismiss Goebbels' statement about an allegedly "natural" clash between two "élites", an old, aristocratic and to some extent degenerate élite and a young one arising from the people with all the signs of high biological quality. Neither is the thesis tenable which was so widespread in Western countries during the war and spoke of a "natural" alliance between "Prussian militarism" and "Nazism". In reality, the problem of this relationship has many complex aspects, it passed through a number of stages and it evades all simplifying terminology.

First, it must be realised that differing conditions prevailed in the individual branches of the armed forces. The German Navy, whose actual development belongs to the days of William II, was always to a higher degree "nationalistic" and to a lesser degree "Prussian" than those military institutions which dated from before the founding of the *Reich* in 1870. In its modern form it was recruited from the whole of Germany; it had an officers' corps in which middle-class elements predominated. This applies even more to the *Luftwaffe* (Air Force) and to the anti-aircraft defence subordinated to it. As a new organisation without traditions it had no roots in historical soil and it naturally held a particular attraction for men with technical interests and a technical education. That paratroops represent a particular sociological group is evident to the contemporary observer of North African events, but the fact is not of any particular political importance in the history of the Third Reich. So far as one can generalise in such matters, it can be said that the Navy and the *Luftwaffe* showed little of the spirit of opposition; they were more imbued with Nazism or with a greater spirit of conformity than the "Prussian" Army with its "aristocratic" officers' corps. While there was one naval Commander (Kranzfelder) among the victims of 20th July, Canaris was the only Admiral among the leading conspirators in the armed forces and he certainly cannot be considered, at any rate in the position he occupied, as a typical naval officer. The conspirators in Goering's Air Ministry were even more outsiders. Moreover, in wartime the Army naturally represented the largest mass organisation and in peace the only one possessing the strength to deal with the Gestapo and the SS. It must be doubted whether, from a purely technical point of view, the *Luftwaffe* could have been used for such purposes. And as far as the Navy was concerned, the differences were clear compared with the situation which gave the sailors' revolutions in Kronstadt or Kiel their significance in 1917 and 1918.

It is therefore on the Army and on the conceptual framework of Prussian and aristocratic traditions associated with it that we must concentrate. So far as this military section of the Third Reich is concerned, there is no doubt that a certain cleavage existed from the start. Whatever the contribution of the Munich *Reichswehr* may have been to the rise of the Party, or that of East Prussian commanders like von Blomberg and von Reichenau to Hitler's seizure of power, their support was not for the National Socialist world of ideas in itself (however much younger officers and activists may have been enamoured of it), but for its exploitation for the purposes of national defence and the revival of military morale. The support was in many cases given with the same reservations maintained by other social groups, both inside and outside Germany. The hope was indulged that the "Drummer", the "Bohemian Corporal", could be used as a tool, to be got rid of when he had done his "duty". This was an illusion which was to have widespread and fateful consequences. But beside the willingness of military opportunists to reach an understanding with Hitler, there were many high-ranking officers who were to act as unqualified opponents. First among them was the Chief of the Army Command from 1930 to 1934, Colonel-General von Hammerstein-Equord—the "red General" as he was often called. He had seen, as he said, no reason "to concern himself with politics" under Schleicher's Chancellorship, but when this was drawing to an end he had intervened with the Reich President, not only apparently against a dictatorial Papen-Hugenberg combination but also against the entry of National Socialists into the Government. This appears from the fact that, though strongly deprecating the interference of the military,

Hindenburg assured Hammerstein that he had no intention of making the Austrian corporal Defence Minister or Reich Chancellor.

The maxim of remaining aloof was more or less consciously the prevailing one during the first few years of the régime. It seemed to be in harmony with Prussian military traditions and with aristocratic caste concepts. But, depending on the situation, the principle of refraining from political activity could cover a wide variety of attitudes. Before 1914, it meant avoidance of interfering in public affairs, which in those days appeared "improper". After 1919, it meant that the German Army formed a kind of State within the State and reserved its own policy. Under conditions created by the Nazi régime, however, the same attitude of "hands off" acquired a completely changed meaning : it meant in practice the toleration of crime and murder by those who possessed the necessary force to prevent them. Thus the traditional maxim of remaining aloof contradicted in this sense another highly honourable military and aristocratic tradition, that of *noblesse oblige* and of a duty to protect the weak.

Certainly, many officers were indignant at the murder of von Schleicher and at the way in which atonement for the deed was evaded, and at the unimaginable intrigues to which their own Commander-in-Chief, von Fritsch, fell a victim, or, in so far as they could not see through the whole matter, at his shameful treatment which no formal rehabilitation could make good. Certainly, many of them were ashamed of the racial laws which hit so many of their comrades or the families of their comrades and which rent asunder the bonds of loyalty with Jewish war veterans or destroyed their position in the national community and often enough their very lives. It may well be that many officers reacted similarly to the brutalities occurring outside the professional military sphere, to the horrors and shameful deeds which they could not fail to hear about or which they observed in the streets. It was perhaps a sign of protest and in any event an unusual sight to see officers attending Divine Service in public in large numbers and in uniform. There is also no doubt that the Army gave support to the Confessing Church and saw the attack on the Christian religion as a threat to the moral basis of soldiership. The handbook of "Military ·Psychology" published at the instance of the Ministry of National Defence stressed this standpoint very strongly, for indeed the whole atmosphere sur-

E

rounding the régime, its boastfulness, its demagogy, its appeal to low instincts, was as "un-Prussian" as could be. And yet no direct resistance or revolt followed from this contrast.

One can very well understand that Colonel-General von Fritsch did not give the sign for a military rebellion when it was a question of his own defence. But there were enough attacks on honour and morality of a general character which might have served as reason for cleaning up the régime. In fact, reports on its crimes were systematically collected by the "Intelligence" in order to have them handy as material for action. But no such opportunity was used. When murder, plunder and burning synagogues disfigured the face of many German towns and the German name in November, 1938, the bonds of discipline proved so strong that no spontaneous military intervention took place, and it was not until the Polish campaign that indignation founded on the genuine military spirit was vented and led to deeds. Regimental Commanders are quoted as having put an end to the pillage and murder of the SS by force of arms. And there is the important testimony of a senior officer, Helmut Stieff, who later became a Major-General, and who under the impact of these and similar experiences was to join the Resistance as a very active member. Confronted with the deeds of "subhumanity", he wrote to his wife : "I am ashamed to be a German." But such attitudes received no sanction from above. Although General von Reichenau protested and the Army Commander, Colonel-General Blaskowitz, demanded official action, nothing was done. And once again, an opportunity to preserve the honour of the German Army was missed.

While these sins of omission must be stated unmistakably it must at the same time be said that the military attitude of "remaining aloof" was also a kind of opposition, in the same sense as this has been noted for other "impenetrable" sections of the population. This applied to the Army in a yet higher degree. It was in fact the only social body within the State as a whole that was in a position and seemed determined to close the pores of infiltration. Soldiers were not allowed to be members of the Party, politics were excluded from military life and the repeated attempts of Dr. Ley to entrust the supervision of the soldiers' spare time to the "Strength Through Joy" Organisation were successfully defeated. Moreover, it was fairly well known that Nazi functionaries who were called to the colours did not exactly enjoy the sergeant's favouritism and that their inflated ideas were usually soon dispelled. An author in exile has rightly said : "The Army never tried to conceal the view that young people who came direct from the Nazi training camps had first to be rid of the greater part of the ideological phrases which had been taught them." In the military schools there was no new-fangled nonsense of this kind. Neither was the pre-military training by the Hitler Youth looked on at all favourably. As an old officer sarcastically remarked : "The only result of the constant marching is distaste for everything military—and flat feet." Often, recruits were preferred who had been members of Socialist youth organisations. "These are the kind of people we want."

Thus in the early years of the régime the Army was to a high degree Nazi-proof. This fact probably strengthened a feeling of self-confidence that was yet to prove an illusion. It was thought possible to await the fruits of Hitler's policy in questions of treaty revision and rearmament without being caught in the maelstrom. Indeed, the Army appeared to be a place of refuge for young people who wanted to keep free of the Party and assure themselves the possibility of resisting inside Germany. On one occasion, when von Hammerstein was told of the increasing numbers of candidates for the higher leaving certificate who were applying for an officer's career he is said to have replied : "I know well that that, too, is a form of inner emigration."

In truth, however, the integrity of the Army was demolished step by step, partly through the fault of its leaders, particularly von Blomberg, and partly owing to Hitler's calculated policy. Hammerstein was dismissed in February, 1934, and the defeat of the SA on 30th June of the same year proved a Pyrrhic victory for the Generals. Not only did the SS reap the success of disposing of a competitor and extending the sphere of its own power, but Röhm's plan of transforming the Reichswehr into a "People's army" by the mass incorporation of the SA and thereby neutralising it came into effect. The plan was carried out by Hitler, though in a different form. The first step was taken in August, 1934, when, a few hours after the death of the Reich President, the Army was obliged to take an oath imposing on it unqualified obedience to the person of the *Führer*. This comprised a moral obligation, however immoral its content, and an impediment that by all traditional standards was not easy to circumvent, even in the case of clearly unlawful orders or of a criminal leadership.

The next step was the reintroduction of compulsory military service in March, 1935. Beck, the friend of Hammerstein, who had been head of the Adjutant General's Department since 1st October, 1933, and, since 1st July, 1935, Chief of the General Staff, opposed this measure, or at least its speed and scope, as a "premature birth". His objections were technical as well as political. He foresaw not only a fall-off in the purely military quality of the Army and an increasing danger of rash adventures, but also a softening and a mass-disorganisation of the basis on which the Nazi-free character of the Army had rested.

In fact, the rapid increase in numbers opened the barriers. It led to the undermining of that aloof position which in normal circumstances might be ambiguous, but under the conditions of the Nazi régime nevertheless included positive possibilities. The sudden increase also meant rapid advancement for young officers and an unusual rate of promotion in the *Führerkorps*. In all this Hitler without doubt pursued a planned policy of bribery. While the fact that the Army was the instrument of a criminal régime was in itself a cause of corruption, the lure of material temptation widened the seat of infection. In many cases the façade of "Prussianism" proved as hollow as other traditions of a more modest and nobler past which themselves had long since become an empty show for broad sections of the German people. In other words, the officers' corps had become just as infected as members of other groups by the materialistic spirit which had spread since the late nineteenth century. One can simply find no connection between the "militaristic spirit" or the "categorical imperative" of an officer caste and the attitude of generals who got the *Führer* to sanction their misalliances or pay their private debts or who later accepted "personal" gifts from him in money or land.

In addition, there were other factors working against the Resistance elements in the Army. On the one hand, Hitler's prestige was increased by the series of surprise successes which seemed to form an unbroken chain from the denunciation of the military clauses of the Versailles Treaty and the re-occupation of the Rhineland (March, 1936), through the incorporation of Austria and the Sudetenland to the occupation of Prague (March, 1939). In each one of these cases Hitler threw the warnings of the Army Command to the wind and every time in the opinion of his international opponents he appeared to score off the military. That increased his self-confidence enormously and undermined the authority of all those who sought to oppose him with their "old-fashioned" ideas. And then, shortly before the entry into Vienna, Hitler dealt the autonomy of the Army a decisive blow. In the course of a treacherous intrigue the War Minister, von Blomberg, who was heavily compromised in his private life, and the Commander-in-Chief of the Army, von Fritsch, whose moral integrity was unimpeachable, were both dismissed. On the 4th February, 1938, Hitler himself assumed personal command of the armed forces. He set up a new unified command, the *Oberkommando der Wehrmacht* (OKW) with a typical yes-man, Keitel, as Chief of the Combined General Staff. At the same time a number of generals (ten to twelve corps and divisional commanders) who had proved refractory were discharged. Most of them bore old Prussian names.

This was the situation in which the Army found itself on the outbreak of war. The defeat which the military section of the revolt experienced on 20th July at the hands of "loyal" officers can be explained to a certain degree though by no means entirely by this softening up of the old framework. It was also one of the contributory factors which underlay the failure of all efforts of the "Sisyphus" work of the Opposition in the years 1939 to 1944. It was Sisyphus work from the point of view of those who urged military action and the historical observer cannot avoid the same impression of "tantalising" effort.

Some few words will suffice to characterise the "Resistance against the Resistance". All witnesses, however different in tone, the Gisevius and Goerdelers, the Hassells and Schlabrendorffs, agree practically in their complaints at the hesitation and evasion shown by Army and Army Group Commanders. Some leading commanders at the front could eventually be won over to the Opposition, above all Field Marshal Rommel. Others had to be worked on for months on end and then they continually slipped back into indecision or failed at the last moment. It would be difficult to decide in individual cases whether such an attitude rested on traditional loyalty or a misconceived patriotism or on weakness of character. Captain Hermann Kaiser, who was on the staff of Colonel-General Fromm, the Commander of the Home Army, and an important liaison officer between Goerdeler and the military Resistance, wrote of the Generals in his diary (20th February, 1943): "One wants to act when he receives orders and the other to give the orders when action starts." This is probably the best and most objective description possible of the average military attitude. Of most of the senior commanders it could be assumed that they would follow the Opposition leaders when it came to a break or, better still, when the bond of their oath to Hitler was abolished by his elimination. But while they were not prepared to commit themselves, neither were they in the least inclined—and this can be checked in numerous cases— to denounce those who sought to persuade them to defect. They were also paralysed by doubt as to how the younger officers would react. The conspirators looked on such an attitude with contempt. Beck is alleged to have declared : "These cowards are trying to make an anti-militarist of me, an old soldier." Hassell inveighed in his diary against the "hopeless sergeants". And Kaiser noted : "One only needs to think of Scharnhorst or Clausewitz or Gneisenau to realise the depths to which the officer of today has sunk."

Goerdeler's letters express the same indignation in biting terms. To General Olbricht, the Deputy Commander of the Home Army who belonged to the circle of conspirators from the beginning, he wrote that it was not a matter of waiting for the "psychologically appropriate" moment, but of bringing it about. He addressed a particularly bitter complaint to Field Marshal von Kluge whose evasive attitude represented a major obstacle. Goerdeler declared that he was no longer in a position to defend Prussian militarism against his friends, particularly in South Germany. For they were men, he wrote, "who have a warm heart for Germany and the German soldier, but who are in despair that with open eyes, a thinking mind and a feeling heart, people can allow Germany to be led into the abyss by criminals and fools, and German youth and German men be driven to death and mutilation without doing anything about it."

Against this background the names of those professional soldiers who were determined to act stand out the more brightly. Although retired, Beck remained among the military and beyond them the secret centre of the will to resist. He came from a middle-class family in the Rhineland and combined a liberal with a strictly scientific mind. He has been described as "one of those rare phenomena in whom the universal education and European amplitude of the eighteenth century were combined with the essential principles of Prussian tradition". In fact he was reminiscent of the intellectually fertile officers of the Prussian reform period after Jena whose names were invoked in Kaiser's diary. Like them, Beck was accounted a military thinker of high standing and his writings confirm this reputation. At the same time, he was deeply rooted in the Christian Faith and anything but a "Militarist". He was in lively contact with the problems of his time far beyond the bounds of his specialised interests. And if senior military circles—and not by any means only his own supporters and pupils—credited him with the ability to show the highest qualities of leadership in case of need, this was not only because of his intellectual clarity, but above all on account of his firmness of character. It was for reasons of character that in 1930 he shielded two second lieutenants in his Ulm regiment who were being prosecuted for National Socialist activity. He would have agreed with another officer (Stieff) who joined the Resistance : "We will do our own dirty washing." As a character he then crossed Hitler's path, not only because his war policy was bound to lead to an annihilating defeat, but because a régime of criminals was in itself destroying the country and its people. On this basic ethical force, on this firmness of soul and strength of mind his resistance was founded. "In total war", he wrote in 1942, "it is no less a question of stressing the ethical postulates of all policy."

No less unusual as a military type was Colonel Graf Claus Schenk von Stauffenberg. After being severely wounded and losing an eye, his right hand and two fingers of the left, he became first assistant of Olbricht in October, 1943, and finally, in June, 1944, Chief of Staff to the Commander-in-Chief of the Home Army. Thereby he obtained a key position which he filled with his own dynamism and which, thanks to the possibilities which it afforded him, led him to become the leading spirit and organisational chief of the conspiracy as well as the perpetrator of the 20th July. A Catholic from a Swabian family, a descendant of Gneisenau on his mother's side, a man of artistic leanings and humanistic education and a member of the select circle round Stefan George, he allowed himself to be carried away by the nationalist tide in 1933, but soon became a radical opponent and an enemy of the totalitarian system in all its manifestations, political, social, cultural and religious. One need only look at his portrait to realise that this was no ordinary cavalry colonel or man of narrow military ambitions, however much he may have distinguished himself as a soldier. In him as in others, the intellectual clarity of a staff officer brought up in the Prussian school combined with purity and spirituality to make him a natural leader in the battle against the dark forces of the age and against every kind of dehumanised policy in war and peace. Through his like-minded cousin, Graf Peter Yorck von Wartenburg and his brother Berthold who was adviser on international law to the High Command of the Navy he was linked to the Kreisau circle. He liked to cite Stefan George's poem on the "Anti-Christ" in which the seer, in an amazing and awesome vision, foresaw the events which now threatened to occur in Germany. In him, as in his close friends, there lived a picture of spiritual, ethical and also social renewal which for the soldier depended on redeeming action: "When once this race has cleansed itself of shame,—and flung from its neck the tyrant's chains..."

But there were plenty of other officers resolved to resist who were soldiers first, and indeed of the normal professional type. Many of them bore old Prussian aristocratic names and an impressive list could easily be drawn up of generals and other officers—colonels, staff officers, captains and lieutenants. A large number of them can be found on the roll of honour of the victims of 20th July. Not a few of them held key positions. The Deputy Commander of the Home Army, General Olbricht, has already been mentioned. Besides Stauffenberg, Colonel Mertz von Quirnheim must be mentioned among his staff officers. Field Marshal von Witzleben, like Colonel-General Hoepner, belonged to the oppositional circle from the start. As we saw, he was ready to act during the crisis of September, 1938, and his attitude remained the same through the years. In the event of Hitler being removed, he was to receive command of the armed forces. In the Supreme Command of the Armed Forces Colonels von Freytag-Loringhoven and Hansen were in the conspiracy and in the Army General Staff, Heusinger, Stieff, Wagner, von Roenne, Fellgiebel and Lindemann—all Heads of Departments. A department "for special employment" headed by Lieutenant-Colonel Grosscurth was entrusted by Halder and Canaris in the winter of 1939 with working up the existing plan for a *coup d'état*. The department was in contact with the Foreign Office through *Legationsrat* von Etzdorf and disseminated material among the higher staffs on the persecution of the Churches and the Jews as well as on SS outrages in Poland.

To what extent front-line commanders were won over to the Opposition cannot be determined with certainty. Certainly it has been rightly said that opposition to Hitler moved in concentric circles of varying thickness. There were differences between those who knew that something was to be undertaken, those who held themselves in readiness in case something happened and those who were not initiated because they could be counted upon to co-operate. But while a healthy scepticism may be maintained towards claims to participation based on no more than a clenched fist in the pocket, in many cases we are on surer ground. The Berlin Garrison Commander, General von Hase, was in the conspiracy, and Olbricht together with Colonel Mertz von Quirnheim and the Quartermaster-General Wagner undertook to fill the commands in other cities with initiates or reliable officers. On the Eastern front the most important conspirator was Major-General Henning von Tresckow, until October, 1943, G.S.O.I. of the Central Army Group. In the words of Schlabrendorff who was particularly close to him, his opposition to Hitler which had existed since long before the war was founded on : "... a distaste for everything which grew from the root of foul play." He threw "his whole personality into the political battle". He succeeded in drawing into his staff a whole group of resolute anti-Nazis, among them von Kleist, von Gersdorff, Graf von Hardenberg and Graf von Lehndorff. He also had confidants on the staff of Army Group South. In the West, the Military Commander in Belgium, General von Falkenhausen, had been won over to the conspiracy at an early stage; he was, however, relieved of his command shortly before 20th July. Above all, General Karl Heinrich von Stülpnagel belonged to the opposition circle. In 1941 he had succeeded his cousin of the same name as Commander-in-Chief in France. A man of universal education and outstanding personality, similar to Beck, he had taken part in the Putsch plans in 1938–39. His staff in Paris, to which Graf v.d. Schulenburg for a time belonged and in which Lieutenant-Colonel Caesar von Hofacker, a cousin of Stauffenberg, was particularly insistent on action and maintained contact with the Berlin group, became a centre of the Resistance. Stülpnagel succeeded in winning over Rommel, finding a resolute helper in his Chief of Staff, General Speidel. It is a paradoxical fact that only in Paris (and to a certain extent in Vienna) did the revolt of 20th July achieve temporary success. A few days before the attempt on Hitler's life,

Hofacker wrote: "Today any unnecessary delay, even of a few hours, would be a sin against the Holy Ghost..." On the code-word "Launched" Stülpnagel ordered the arrest of the Paris Gestapo and of the heads of the Security Service and the SS, and this took place without a hitch.

Here then the question may be asked, how, despite the participation or preparedness of so many officers in key positions, all military plans for action finally miscarried. A partial explanation lies in the fact that, with the possible exception of those in the Information and Intelligence Services, Prussian military personnel had been poorly trained for the work of conspiracy. There was no revolutionary tradition such as had existed—and in the general view not exactly as a claim to fame—in the armies of Southern Europe and Latin America.

Another explanation suggests itself and has been widely accepted; Nazi supporters or vacillating non-Nazis frustrated all attempts. To a certain degree this is true. As we have already said, a good deal of the conspirators' energy was consumed in a veritable labour of Sisyphus: the stone kept rolling down the hill again. Thus in November, 1939, the plan of action failed because, amongst other reasons, von Brauchitsch abstained. And the Commander of the Home Army, Colonel-General Fromm, was more than uncertain in his attitude. And most of the commanders in the field observed a kind of wait-and-see neutrality. Weighty arguments should be adduced for doing so. Could they risk starting a new stab-in-the-back legend and one which, this time, would be directed against the officers' corps? How could the German people and the German Army be convinced that Hitler was leading them to destruction while the way to victory still seemed open? And conversely, under the threat of imminent defeat, how could the catastrophe be hastened or made yet more disastrous by revolutionising the front? In his statement at the Weizsäcker trial General Halder expressed his conception of this dilemma in a somewhat different fashion. In external politics, he said, a military success was the prerequisite for a successful revolt, in internal politics, a reverse. We have seen that Goerdeler spoke cuttingly of waiting for the "right psychological moment" and it can be assumed that this waiting and the reasons put forward for it were in fact a means of evading a decision.

But within the purely military sphere of thought there was hardly a way out of the dilemma. And one can well understand that in the later years the commanders of fighting troops, particularly of those in the East which formed a dam against a system certainly no more humane than that of the Nazis, decided on grimly holding out. The men of the German military Resistance would certainly have been the last to deny the respect which is eternally due to the spirit of comradeship and self-sacrifice in which their sons, relatives and friends lived and to the illusionless fulfilment of a harsh duty as it was practised day-in, day-out at the front. That the staffs in rear of the front left it in the lurch or sabotaged its supplies or that treason contributed to the collapse of the Central Army Group is simply not true. The problem of sabotage as it is treated by Zuckmayer in the person of his engineer Oderbruch is shown in too harsh a light and is oversimplified. But the moral question involved here had another dimension. The deepest thinkers were convinced that under the existing régime a German victory was not even desirable. That victory was improbable, even in the outward triumph of the early years, and became increasingly so is beyond question; it is also undeniable that the situation was completely hopeless when the rising finally took place and therefore the opposition could not have "brought about" the defeat of the Fatherland; nevertheless, this should not blind us to the severity of the conflict which in the nature of things confronted a military Opposition seeking the downfall of its own government in the midst of war. Some officers of high ethical standards—like von Fritsch or the German commander at Cherbourg—sought death on the battlefield as the only honourable solution to a tragic dilemma. For their part, the conspirators naturally wanted to avoid a split in the Army or open civil war. They thought in terms of a "blitz revolution" to be carried out with united armed force. The consequence was that, as had been the case before September, 1939, a number of valid psychological moments—prior to the attack on France, for instance, or during and after Stalingrad—were missed.

But this reference to obstacles and inhibitions still does not supply a full explanation. It is an undeniable fact that many actions were planned although they lacked the support of high commanders. And the reason for their failure was not spineless neutrality or the existence of a Resistance against the Resistance. Instructions worked out in August and September, 1943, for the "Day"—the code-word was "Valkyrie"—presupposed Hitler's death as an accomplished fact. The orders imposed a state of siege during the period in which executive power would rest with the new Commander-in-Chief, von Witzleben. It would be delegated to the generals commanding the Home Army and the Occupation Armies. SS troops were to be disarmed and if necessary suppressed by force. Concentration camps were to be occupied by the Army, and so forth. One of these orders was signed by von Witzleben "without hesitation", the other bore the name of Colonel-General Fromm, though he was not an initiate, and in addition Stauffenberg's signature. Both orders were typed by Frau von Tresckow and a former secretary of Hammerstein's, Fräulein von Oven. They were taken over—sealed—by Olbricht for safe keeping. One cannot say that this concern with fictions was a very orthodox military procedure, but it showed that little regard was paid to obstacles or obstructive personalities. The same can be said of a number of other attempts which came near to execution and whose failure had simply nothing to do with the attitude of neutrals or Nazi conformists.

The first who was prepared to act, and act at the moment of military triumph, was von Hammerstein. During the Polish campaign he commanded Army Corps "A" on the North Rhine front. Hitler was persuaded to demonstrate German strength in the West by paying a visit to this front and Hammerstein was determined to arrest him as soon as he appeared. But Hitler had one of his "premonitions"; the visit was cancelled and then Hammerstein was relegated to retirement. A far more urgent form was assumed by Resistance plans in November, 1939, after the end of the Polish campaign and before the offensive in the West. Among the Army-Group Commanders in the West, Colonel-General von Leeb, also Halder and up to a certain point Brauchitsch raised strong objections to starting the campaign in the winter, first because it would be premature, but also from the moral and political point of view as representing fresh aggression and infringement of neutrality. Once again a *coup d'état* was planned in which Lieutenant-Colonel Grosscurth, already mentioned, was to be employed. It was coupled—"in order to release the Generals from their scruples"—with the first concrete plan to assassinate Hitler, and for this task Erich Kordt offered himself because he had entry to the Reich Chancellery. The two liaison officers with the military, von Etzdorf and von Kessel, were also drawn into the plot. On 11th November, the explosive material was to be delivered to Kordt by the Intelligence (Oster), but on the 8th the attempt in the Burgerbräu cellar took place and the resulting increased restrictions made delivery impossible, while on the military side Halder reached an analysis of the situation which prevented him taking the decisive step. During the following months up to the invasion of France the main action lay with the politicians and the leading group in the Intelligence. They sought to obtain assurances from the Allies against revengeful peace terms and for a temporary halt in military operations when the *coup d'état* occurred so as to enable the military to act. We will return to this later in another context.

During the next phase the initiative came from the Eastern front. Increasingly the military were beginning to overcome their religious and moral scruples against killing Hitler. Goerdeler had urged that Hitler should be brought to trial and was only with difficulty persuaded that it was necessary to do away with him. But the soldiers stressed that it was no longer possible to capture Hitler alive owing to the continually increasing security measures and that it was essential to release the Army from its oath of allegiance to him. But they also knew that the initial spark would have to be followed by planned military action and that this would have to be worked out in detail beforehand. This part of the task fell to Olbricht and his staff. It is reported that he finished it towards the end of February, 1943, and the already mentioned sealed orders were deposited in the autumn of that year. To arrange for the initial spark devolved upon Tresckow. Being unable to win over the Commander of the Central Army Group, von Kluge, he decided to act on his own responsibility, though in close concert with the Intelligence. On 13th March, 1943, Schlabrendorff succeeded after careful preparation in smuggling a time-bomb into Hitler's aircraft. But the mechanism proved defective. Some days later, the attempt was repeated during the opening of an exhibition in the Berlin arsenal. Von Gersdorff, who was in Tresckow's confidence, declared himself ready to make use of this opportunity. According to his own statement, he had a time-bomb in each pocket of his overcoat. But Hitler left the exhibition after eight minutes, while the delayed action fuses were set for twenty minutes.

Despite these disappointing failures and ever more stringent security measures, the attempts were not abandoned. Schlabrendorff speaks of plans for a combined attempt in which he and six other officers of Tresckow's staff were to take part. But Hitler never visited the Central Army Group again. When in December of that year Schlabrendorff managed to smuggle a bomb past the security guards the conference in Hitler's headquarters was abandoned at the last moment. A further opportunity seemed to offer when Hitler was due to inspect new uniforms in January, 1944. A plan was evolved by General Stieff and three of Tresckow's officers agreed to make the attempt. One of them was Major von der Bussche and another, a son of Ewald von Kleist. But an air raid prevented the inspection and it was indefinitely postponed.

At last, in July, 1944, the final attempt was undertaken by Stauffenberg. But this, too, was ill fated. It was unfortunate from the start that the "chief of staff" of the conspiracy had to commit the deed himself because only he had access to the *Führerhauptquartier*. Moreover, owing to Goering's and Himmler's absence he had to postpone the attempt twice before he finally made it on 20th July. And once again, Hitler escaped. The effect of the explosion was fatally weakened by a number of circumstances, in particular by the transference of the conference from Hitler's concrete shelter to a wooden barrack.

Surveying these events, one cannot avoid the conclusion that the whole series of failures was due to no other mishap than a barely credible succession of trivial incidents. Hitler might well speak of the "hand of Providence" and in a certain sense the historian will be inclined to agree with him—not with the boastful overtones in which the *Führer's* hysteria discharged itself but in the sense of reverence for the inexplicable. In the chain of events from 1939 to 1945 there seems to be an iron logic, an inner striving towards an unmitigated and inevitable catastrophe which makes the trivial and the incidental unimportant. And yet mishaps played an evident role. They were in part caused or made possible by Hitler's suspicious caution, but they had simply no connection with caution, hesitation or lack of resolve on the part of the officers concerned. In truth, lack of success can never or at any rate should never be a final criterion of judgement.

But another, critical question arises here: what, even if the attempt on Hitler's life had been successful, could the result of the ensuing military Putsch have been? The answer is that the action was in no way a purely military one. Both its motives and its aims were in the political and moral sphere. This study is therefore not concerned with the various oppositional impulses among the Field Marshals and other senior officers who criticised

Hitler's "intuitions" from a sense of professional superiority and who sought here and there (as opposed to Keitel and Jodl) to avert disaster. They might talk indignantly of "that fellow" but that implied no resistance in any basic sense. Neither do the various attempts which were made to remove Hitler from military command concern us here. Even a personality like General Georg Thomas, Chief of the Production and Armament Division of the War Ministry, who was undoubtedly a genuine opponent and a participant in early plans for revolt, has for the later years only a loose connection with the main theme of this book. As an expert on all questions of military preparedness he was opposed to the Hitlerite adventure from the start. Moreover he knew the resources of Russia well enough to side with Beck and his warning prophesies. As chief of military production he was also in particularly close contact with men of the civil Opposition. At the beginning of 1940, he urged the Generals to refuse to attack Belgium and Holland; the Berlin garrison would then arrest Hitler and the Army take over. He continued to stress the necessity of an early end to the war until his discharge towards the end of 1942. But the type of resistance he represented was obviously directed more against a policy that must lead to defeat than against the régime as such. And although his warnings against an attempt on Hitler's life that would make the *Führer* into a martyr were based on conscientious objections that were shared by others and were not unfounded from the point of view of political tactics, it is here that a fine but sharp dividing line appears.

The line was drawn with sure instinct by Tresckow when he said in the summer of 1944 : "The attempt on Hitler's life must take place at any cost. If it does not succeed, the *coup d'état* must nevertheless be attempted. For what matters is no longer the practical object, but that before the world and history the German Resistance movement should have staked its life on risking the decisive throw. Compared with this nothing else matters." Of course, those military men who agreed that action was essential, even if need be without prospect of success, were also concerned to prevent Germany being bled white. They were conscious of acting for their Fatherland, but also against a danger which threatened the whole of Europe with chaos. In the last resort they were concerned to avert a moral crisis and for that purpose they were convinced that they would have to act themselves and if necessary sacrifice themselves. We have seen that soldiers opposed war in 1938 not merely because it would be disastrous for Germany but because, in facing and fighting against this danger, they seemed to have an opportunity of overthrowing a criminal régime and returning to concepts of national and international decency which were in closer accord with genuine military and aristocratic traditions.

This was an attitude which lost none of its validity even in wartime. For those with the strongest and most virile characters the spectre of the "stab-in-the-back" and the accusation of high treason paled before it. When the attempt of 20th July had failed and Tresckow was about to return to the front to take his own life there, he parted from Schlabrendorff with the words: "Now the whole world will fall upon us and load us with abuse. But I am still firmly convinced that we did right. I consider Hitler to be not only the arch-enemy of Germany, but of the world. When I appear before God's Judgement Seat in a few hours' time to account for my actions and omissions, I believe I can stand up with a good conscience for what I have done in the battle against Hitler. Just as God once promised Abraham that he would not destroy Sodom if ten just men could be found there, so I hope that for our sake God will not destroy Germany. None of us can complain at dying. Those who entered our circle donned the shirt of Nessus. A man only begins to show his moral value when he is ready to die for his convictions." Another military conspirator, Graf Lehndorff-Steinort, wrote in his farewell letter to his wife: "You can always be sure that I have not wantonly destroyed your future but have served an idea which I believe does not allow consideration for family and private interests." "The way to the heavenly kingdom", continues the letter, "does indeed lead only through suffering and first one must tear oneself forcibly away from the old life. Only then can one become a 'new creature'. I, at any rate, will die in this faith and without fear or anxiety..."

These, then, were the thoughts and motives which were alive in the members of that "ambitious clique" which allegedly only sought to escape the consequences of the war when it was lost. One recalls with shame that these men were suspected of having sought to save their own lives, or their class interests, or to preserve the General Staff for another war. The case of the German Military Intelligence was even more unconventional and in even sharper contradiction to the thesis that the German Resistance

was composed of dissatisfied generals and "anachronistic" aristocrats. Its head, Admiral Canaris, foresaw as early and as clearly
as anyone the disaster to which aggressive war would finally lead.
His warning has been perpetuated in an Italian document of the
middle of August, 1939 : "This will mean the end of Germany."
At the same time, however, precise knowledge of Hitler's methods
and aims convinced him that his triumph would if possible be
"an even greater misfortune". By nature more inclined to conspiratorial resistance than to revolutionary action, Canaris did not
himself take up direct opposition to the régime, but he informed
and covered others, saved persecuted individuals and mitigated
excesses. Weizsäcker who was close to him says in his memoirs
that he was accounted a "cunning Odysseus" and yet he testifies
that his character was "as sound as a bell". There can be no
doubt of his attitude or of his moral will-power and yet, because
of the gaps in the evidence, his historical role remains to a certain
extent shrouded in mystery. His Chief of Staff on the other hand,
Major-General Oster, is a clear-cut figure. Schlabrendorff said
of him that he was "a man after God's heart". Oster was not
merely the "technician" who covered up the conspiracy and
maintained most valuable contacts. He was himself one of the
main driving forces and he did not shrink from actions which
might have caused severe damage to the Germany Army.

It is at this point that we must clearly define our attitude to
the question of "treason" within the context of the German Opposition. We cannot content ourselves with the thesis of the
"wrongful" character of a régime towards which, therefore, no
wrong can be done, whatever the welcome divergence of this
conception from that of juridical positivism. Neither can the
problem be minimised by referring to the fact that the information
which Oster gave the Dutch Military Attaché, G. J. Sas, concerning the dates of the impending attacks on Denmark, Norway,
Belgium and Holland did no harm because apparently it was not
believed and, in the case of Holland, precautionary measures had
in any event been taken. Neither does reference to the diplomatic
and tactical situation suffice or to the soundings made by the
Opposition among the Allies with the object of achieving a military standstill during the period of the internal revolt. Certainly
it was necessary to prove that the Opposition was in earnest about
this. But undoubtedly Oster acted both from feelings of indignation and European solidarity and also with the aim of avoiding

F

a total defeat for his country by incurring a smaller military reverse which would make it possible to overthrow the régime. The
question whether passing on the date of a projected attack was
not an unsuitable means to this end and the "deed" was therefore
superfluous does not do justice to a break-through which could
only come from the conscience—a break through the professional
ethics of an officer and his, as it were, normal patriotism which
was imposed on the military sector as a whole, even if in less
extreme forms. The Oster case should therefore be considered not
as a superfluous, but as a very valid evidence of the scale of values
which are and may again be brought to bear in critical situations.

If the problem is thus thought out to its conclusion and applied
from this border-line case to the whole, including the more
average phenomena of military opposition, a picture emerges
which has little connection with that of a war-mongering General
Staff, but reveals it rather in decisive phases and decisive personalities as a very "civilian" advocate of peace and of a rightfully
ordered community of peoples. Perhaps the contrast with certain
caricatured conceptions can best be pointed by a quotation from
Hitler which Schlabrendorff has reported: "Before I became
Reich Chancellor, I believed that the General Staff was like a
mastiff that had to be held firmly by the collar as otherwise it
would threaten to attack everyone. Since becoming Reich Chancellor I have been forced to the conclusion that the General Staff
is anything but a mastiff. This General Staff has always tried to
prevent me doing what I held to be necessary. The General Staff
opposed rearmament, the occupation of the Rhineland, the entry
into Austria, the occupation of Czechoslovakia and finally the
war against Poland. The General Staff advised me against taking
the offensive against France and making war on Russia. It is I
who always have to incite this mastiff."

It may then be said in conclusion that the motives of the military Opposition, in so far as they concern us here, were neither
of a purely professional nor of a class-conditioned kind. The same
applies to their aims. The Resistance movement in the Army was
a sector, was part of the whole. And though it embraced some of
the best Prussian traditions, "civilian" ideas evidently predominated in it and remained decisive to the end. It is worth mention-
ing in this connection that on the staff of the Home Army and
in the circle round Canaris and Oster—in the two places where
the number of conspirators was greatest—the percentage of

reserve officers and civilians was likewise very high. Lawyers, judges, teachers, professors, farmers, business men and churchmen all had a part in the military planning : the brothers Kaiser and Bonhoeffer, Justus Delbrück and Hans von Dohnanyi, a brother-in-law of the Bonhoeffers. While Oster worked on the military side, Dohnanyi was used in the political preparation of the coup within the framework of the Intelligence. Closely connected with them was another brother-in-law of the Bonhoeffers, Dr. R. Schleicher, and Dr. Karl Sack, Freiherr von Guttenberg, Graf von Schwerin-Schwanenfeld, Strünck and Dr. O. John, who, like Klaus Bonhoeffer, had particular opportunities owing to a position in the Lufthansa. Co-operation between the military and the civilian sector was also very close. While representatives of Beck and the Intelligence attended discussions in political circles—as we shall illustrate later by a concrete example—leaders of the political Right and of the Left conferred with the military conspirators and gave them their advice. Some civilians like Goerdeler and von Hassell made continual and desperate efforts to drive reluctant generals forward. But it seems there were others who sought to delay rather than to hasten military action. According to existing testimony, at the end of 1942 three of the younger Socialist leaders sought to persuade the Generals to postpone the attempt on Hitler's life until the Western Allies had landed on the Continent. In their opinion, a premature attempt involving the fall of the German Government would mean conquest by Russia and a Communist inundation of all Europe. Assuming this view was accepted, it might help to explain a certain pause which occurred in the military action. At any event, the international effect of an attempt on Hitler's life entered very much into the discussions, as will be shown later. From this point, too, the basically political character of the military Opposition appears.

It therefore represented a very justified, though rather exhaustive conclusion when Gustav Dahrendorf, one of the few survivors among the leading Socialist conspirators, said later : "The revolutionary coup of 20th July, 1944, should not be considered a badly executed undertaking ، on the part of officers who had given up all hope and sought to escape from an exigency. Neither was it an attempt by grumbling reactionary militarists to cut the bond which tied them to Fascism. Both descriptions would be false and unjust. The motivating force which underlay all preparations was a firm political will. There was only one aim, to remove Fascism and end the war." The military revolt was in fact only the first, although an indispensable step towards this goal. It comprised "the fighting vanguard of the Resistance movement...but determined neither its body nor its soul". The state of siege under military control which was planned was only thought of as a temporary emergency measure. Civilians and soldiers together had worked out drafts for a new constitutional government, for the restoration of the rule of law, for religious freedom, for political and social reform.

Our study has now to turn to this side of the problem, that is, to the political structure and the political and social aims of the Opposition.

4. Political Structure of the Opposition

Among the non-military leaders of the Opposition Carl Friedrich Goerdeler stands out as a personality. It is he also who has left behind a large number of programmes and draft reforms for the post-Hitler government. They do not express a body of thought common to the Resistance movement as a whole, but they provide a first and comparatively broad basis for an assessment of its ideas and aims.

A West Prussian by birth, in the years preceding the Nazi régime Goerdeler had distinguished himself by personal initiative and a sense of political responsibility to a degree which was not exactly the rule for a senior civil servant, even in the sphere of local government. We have mentioned that besides being Oberburgermaster of Leipzig he was for a time (1934 to 1935) a Price Commissar under Hitler. In this position he tried in vain to exert a moderating influence. Like other unimpeachable opponents of National Socialism he held it his duty not to retire at once or leave the country. But he certainly refused to compromise his principles. When he failed to prevent a Party anti-Semitic demonstration in Leipzig (the removal of the Mendelssohn memorial in November, 1936) he resigned his office. He then became adviser in Stuttgart to Robert Bosch, one of the socially most progressive of German industrial *entrepreneurs*. Bosch supplied him with the money and, what was more important, with the cover which his widespread activity in combating the régime required. Goerdeler's contacts extended practically to all non-Communist groups in the Opposition. Many of them had their rallying point in him. He was, of course, in close contact with the military and with men of the business world, with retired senior civil servants and with serving members of the Foreign Office, but also with professors and churchmen (particularly with the Bishop of Berlin, Graf Preysing, and the Protestant Bishop Wurm of Württemberg) as well as with Socialist and trade union leaders. Moreover, he had many friends abroad; he travelled repeatedly through Britain and France, Italy and Switzerland, Sweden and Belgium, the Near East and Balkan countries, the United States and Canada. Before the war he undoubtedly did all in his power to convince the outside world of the danger inherent in the character of the Nazi régime.

In 1937, while staying in the United States, Goerdeler deposited a "Political Testament" with one of his friends. This document not only shows that he was well aware of the abyss towards which he himself and the whole German people were drifting; it also shows that he was alarmed above all by the lawlessness and corruption, the breakdown of justice and the attacks on Christianity and that he saw in these phenomena the essentials of a system to which foreigners were still inclined to give credit for some economic achievements. As an expert in administration and finance he did not belong to those who allowed themselves to be dazzled by apparent successes. Long before the war he was convinced that even without a war Hitler would lead Germany to an economic and above all a moral catastrophe. In his opinion, the dictatorship drew its strength from the very roots of the disease which had befallen the age. In April, 1938, he wrote an article attacking the materialistic outlook ·of the epoch as its "great mistake". Freedom from this slavery, he declared, "can only be won by the utmost exertion of the moral forces which God has given to Man".

In fact it was more from this viewpoint than from any other that Goerdeler began and continued his agitation. He was concerned to see the basic values of human existence restored. He sought tirelessly to convince the Generals of the danger of the complete moral chaos that would result from the continuation of a cynical régime of criminal brutality. And he did not spare references to their particular responsibility for such a collapse. They had looked on, he told them, while the principle of universal military service had been robbed of its ethical content and made an instrument of egotistic and criminal aims. He did not consider honour and decency as so much "scrap iron", but as the springs, as he expressed it, of "that living strength which every community requires for its existence, particularly one which demands the highest sacrifices". In a detailed memorandum entitled "Situation and Possibilities" which Goerdeler addressed to a group of generals on 26th March, 1943, he came to the conclusion that there should be only one dividing line in Germany, "that between decent and non-decent". He also raised the same question that was so often asked with a slightly different stress abroad: "How is it possible that so basically decent a people as the Germans can put up for so long with such an intolerable system?" His answer was: "Only because all offences against law and decency are carried out under the protection of secrecy and under the pressure of terror...." The practical task, he wrote, was to bring about a situation "in which, if only for twenty-four hours, it is possible to allow truth to be spoken again". To bring about this situation was a matter for a "resolute man of action". "The people are not only ripe for an act of salvation, they expect it." Barely two months later, Goerdeler wrote the letter to Olbricht already mentioned which complained about waiting for the "psychological moment" and ended with the surprising suggestion that he himself would tell Hitler in an interview "that his resignation is required by the vital interests of the German people". First, however, he demanded an assurance that "action will take place immediately afterwards".

There can be no doubt of the courage and readiness for self-sacrifice implicit in such words: they were certainly not intended as a means of bringing tactical pressure to bear, but were a genuine expression of personality. At the same time, they missed the reality of the situation to the extent that it could not be mastered by "decent means". In fact it will be seen that, although a man of wide practical knowledge and year-long schooling in the sphere of municipal self-government, Goerdeler all too readily indulged in idealistic simplifications and excessive optimism. Often enough his fellow conspirators had cause to complain of these characteristics. But nobody could or can deny that they were rooted in the optimism of a faith which took spiritual rather than material forces into account. And they proved to be an irrepressible motive power.

Another leading figure among the non-military conspirators was the former Ambassador in Rome, Ulrich von Hassell, who joined the active Opposition after his dismissal at the end of 1937.

He was the son-in-law of Tirpitz and was descended from an aristocratic Hanover family of civil servants and professors; thus he may be called a representative of the "old élite". He was full of contempt for the upstarts and indignant at their stupid and arrogant blunders: a diplomat who still lived in the genuine Bismarck tradition—however much it had been caricatured. It was unfortunate, wrote Hassell, that in Germany itself a picture had been painted of Bismarck as "the power-politician in cuirassier's boots—in reality his greatest gift was supreme diplomacy and moderation". In personality and cultural background Hassell was certainly as far removed as possible from the revolutionary or conspiratorial type. His diaries, whose existence is as surprising as their survival, prove that amply. No Gestapo men would have found it difficult to decipher them or to find in them everything he could possibly want. At the same time, the diaries reveal the scope of Hassell's intellectual interests and of an activity in Germany and abroad which, like Goerdeler's, was camouflaged by an industrial undertaking. They also supply information concerning his negotiations with enemy go-betweens and his numerous contacts with oppositional elements from almost all circles. He moved by no means only in "higher society", however distinguished his personality appears from all written and pictorial evidence. Rather it must be said that in the foreign policy which he pursued for the Resistance movement he was under some illusion as to what could be achieved and that his ideas were strongly influenced by the picture of a better past.

In the first years after the war it was therefore not unusual abroad—and still is today east of the Iron Curtain—to see in Hassell the specific example of a man who was "hopelessly out of date" or to characterise him as "an anachronism in the modern world".

There was a tendency also to deride "high-handed Junkers who fought Hitler with diaries". This no longer needs refutation. In truth it was anything but an anachronism that an aristocrat such as von Hassell certainly was, though of the West German, not of the Junker type, should read Dante in the midst of a great world crisis or say of Werner Jaeger's *Paideia* that it was a book with surprising insights into antiquity and the future. To all those who see an encouraging symptom in Europe's return to humanist and Christian traditions Hassell amongst others may testify to the seeds which were sown in the time of chaos. Moreover, the diaries mirror perhaps better than any other available document the driving force of horror which was present in people of all classes, but was expressed by Hassell with the particular sensitiveness of the cultivated aristocrat. In the clearest fashion he declared that he shared responsibility for the terrible crimes that were committed in the name of Germany and he urged that this shame should be made good, often enough with the incaution of the nobleman who pays no heed to danger. With the same composure, even nonchalance, he awaited his arrest after 20th July. In so far as he can be called class-bound it was in the sense that he strove to revive and put into force the abandoned motto of *noblesse oblige*.

Many big landowners and members of the nobility were in the same camp: the former Ambassador in Moscow, Graf Werner von der Schulenberg, Pomeranian Junkers like von Zitzewitz-Muttrin and von Puttkammer-Nippoglense, or a farmer and high bailiff in the Prussian province of Saxony, Wenzel-Teutschental, or Graf Dohna-Tolksdorf, who was intended by the conspirators to be their political representative in East Prussia. Many such men of the Right had opposed Hugenberg's course in the years preceding the Nazi régime. An outstanding member of the Conservative Opposition within the landed aristocracy whom we have already mentioned several times was Ewald von Kleist-Schmenzin. In his trial before the People's Court in January, 1945, he declared: "I consider this battle to have been commanded by God. Only God will be my judge." And in some final notes before his death he wrote: "Who is greater, who has done more for the world: Caesar, or a simple, conscientious workman whose whole life was a model of a religious human being?..."

The efforts and the death of such men were not determined by class interests, but reveal a revolt of individuals who followed the genuine commandments of Conservative thought and Christian piety. Beside them the active or retired officials of municipal administration who worked with Goerdeler should be named: his brother Fritz, latterly treasurer of Königsberg, who shared the fate of execution with him, and Doctors Elsas and Lehr; jurists like Friedrich Justus Perels, the legal adviser of the Confessing Church, and the Catholic lawyers Dr. Wirmer and Joseph Müller. One or other of the loosely connected groups also included individuals who had been active in the leadership of the Liberal-Conservative, the Democratic and the Centre Parties.

Amongst them were the former Reichstag deputy Lejeune-Jung, the former ministers Gessler and Hermes, the former State President of Württemberg, Bolz; further, a number of retired senior civil servants such as Freiherr von Lüninck who had been *Oberpräsident* of Westphalia, and two former secretaries of state in the Reich Chancellory, Hamm and Planck. Other members of the same circle have already been mentioned and further names could easily be added to the list of high-placed persons in public life.

Amongst them the Prussian Finance Minister, Johannes Popitz, deserves special mention, not only because his specific contribution to the Opposition is controversial, but because he was without doubt one of the biggest brains in its ranks. He was a man of personal integrity and humanistic education, a respected scientist in the field of political and financial economy who had also made his name as an archaeologist. He had acquired a reputation in the theory and practice of administration after 1918, particularly under the Socialist Finance Minister Hilferding. After a rapid promotion he was for a time a professor at Berlin University. In 1932 he took over the Prussian Finance Ministry and remained in that office after Hitler had come to power. Like other expert administrators, experience taught him that the hope of "avoiding worse" was not to be realised. Without doubt he was a bitter enemy of the régime at least after 1938, deeply concerned at the spreading corruption and determined on resistance from within. After the outbreak of war he, too, was convinced that the end would be disastrous and that no peace would be possible under Hitler and Ribbentrop. Initiated by Goerdeler, he had a part in the attempts to prevent the attack in the West by a military revolt. He was in more or less close contact with Hassell, Schacht and Oster. On the other hand despite many human affinities, he was separated from Goerdeler by a basic difference (to which we shall revert) in his conception of the State and of society. It was probably this which also kept Popitz at a distance from the trade union wing of the Opposition. To this side, as apparently to Goerdeler and Beck, his long stay in the Government was also a cause of distrust. On the other hand, his advocacy of a carefully thought-out reconstruction of the State as well as his preference for a kind of planned economy and for certain state-socialist measures appear to have won him support among the younger generation in the Resistance, particularly in the Kreisau circle.

However that may be, Popitz reached the conviction that the Generals were not to be counted on—"they think only of their medals", he said. Apparently in despair, he canvassed the plan of overthrowing the régime by splitting its forces, i.e. by a palace revolution or a "revolt of the Pretorian guard". And in fact, besides the military Putsch these are the two typical, but also the most hazardous methods of destroying a dictatorship. After Popitz had tried to bring Goering under his influence, not without occasional success, he finally placed his hopes on Himmler, who since 1943 had amongst other things been Reich Minister of the Interior. On this curious episode A. W. Dulles has first reported on the basis of information supplied to him by Marie-Louise Sarre, the daughter of the well-known archaeologist who was herself involved in much conspiratorial activity. A chance find also put into Dulles' hands the indictment against Popitz and his adviser, the lawyer, Dr. Langbehn. Apart from many debatable details, this document at least confirms the fact that Popitz had a conversation with Himmler at the end of August, 1943. It circled cautiously round the theme of reducing the powers of the *Führer*, of "relieving the strain" on him as Reich Chancellor or Commander-in-Chief and of placing men in his entourage who were capable of conducting foreign negotiations. It is known from other sources that during the last phase of the war Himmler tried to play on both sides, particularly under the influence of Schellenberg. But these symptoms of a disintegrating régime do not concern us here and in the framework of a study on the German Opposition care should be taken not to attach too much weight to the Popitz-Himmler episode merely because a chance find has cast so vivid a light on it. It was an entirely isolated sideline. Beck and Tresckow seem to have known about it and would certainly have welcomed a split in the Nazi camp; Goerdeler also knew of the plan but wanted nothing to do with it and was appalled at the extent of the revelations made to Himmler. One may pay full tribute to Langbehn's and Popitz's personal courage, to their temerity, even; it may be recognised that they made use of their access to Goering and Himmler to save the lives or freedom of a number of people. But their separate action was doomed to failure. Within a month, Bormann, the head of the Party and Himmler's rival, was on their trail and Langbehn was arrested in September. The second conversation between Popitz and Himmler was planned but never took place. Popitz himself remained at liberty until the wave of arrests after 20th July made it possible to include him in the general category of conspirators. In view of his conversation with Himmler and on instructions from the Security Service the Reich Ministry of Justice applied special precautions to his and Langbehn's trial. It remained an isolated case.

Schacht, too, cannot properly be included among the political leaders of the Resistance. From 1936 he was undoubtedly an active member of the Opposition, and particularly after his dismissal from office in 1939. But his reputation for ambition, vanity and opportunism excluded him from full partnership. Apparently the leaders of the conspiracy held him at a distance. In so far as the source material allows such a dividing line to be drawn, he took part in none of the meetings at which members of different oppositional groups were present. In retrospect he has taken pride in stressing that he was his "own circle"; that will hardly have been due solely to his own wilfulness. At any rate, no place for him was reserved in any of the plans for a "shadow government".

A very different state of affairs prevailed among leading conspirators of the Left. They played their full part in preparations for the coup and would have shared equal responsibility once the régime was overthrown.

Among the labour leaders Wilhelm Leuschner deserves first mention. Since 1929 he had been Minister of the Interior in Hesse, and since 1932 deputy chairman of the *Allgemeiner Deutscher Gewerkschaftsbund,* the General German Trade Union Alliance. After spending two years in a concentration camp, he set up a small factory in Berlin which not only gave him a living and funds for agitation, but also enabled him to employ a number of reliable colleagues and friends. He travelled about as an inconspicuous business man or sent out "commercial travellers" who restored contacts between the cells of the trade union movement and also with the British trade unions. To their General Secretary he wrote in August, 1939: "We are prisoners in one great house of correction. To rebel would be just as much suicide as if prisoners were to rise against their heavily armed guards."

In clear recognition of this situation, Leuschner was an ideal co-ordinator between the labour movement and the military. His factory produced a special kind of beer tap which had been invented by Schneppenhorst, also a trade union leader and a victim of 20th July. Soon the military began to take an unusual interest in this article. It is reported that Colonel-General Beck used often to visit the factory disguised in dark glasses. According to Pechel, Olbricht supplied the "travellers" with special permits. Leuschner himself, a wood-engraver by profession and a man of outstanding skill and great tenacity, must have had the gift of inspiring confidence in all those who came in contact with him or who struck a chord of sympathy. His pseudonym was "Uncle" and von Hammerstein, the "red General", treated him as an old friend.

Indeed, before Hitler's seizure of power there had already been possibilities of an alliance between the leaders of the trade unions and the Reichswehr. Erwin Planck, son of the famous physicist and secretary of the Reich Chancellery under Schleicher, had worked for such a front and may again have been active to the same end as a go-between. With Goerdeler, too, there was soon close co-operation. Pechel reports that he brought about the first meeting between Goerdeler and Leuschner and also with his colleague, Hermann Maas, the former chairman of the Socialist youth organisations. From 1941 there was close co-operation between them. They agreed on common action and apparently not only for the negative purpose of overthrowing the régime. Beyond that, their accord rested on similar convictions, mutual respect, the absence of personal ambition and, to all appearances, on a considerable measure of agreement in political and social aims. Hassell characterised this rapprochement in his own terms when he remarked in his diary that the "national note" was clearly present with Leuschner and his friends and that wide circles in the former Social Democratic Party held views which were "friendly to Christianity".

The religious character of the Opposition was naturally most strongly marked among the Christian trade unions. Their leader, Jakob Kaiser, was also in close contact with von Hammerstein and had worked with Dr. Brüning in the days preceding Hitler's seizure of power. He was connected with men like Bernhard Letterhaus, a former member of the Prussian Diet and at intervals of the Intelligence in the rank of Captain, with Nikolaus Gross, a former miner, Heinrich Koerner and Franz Leuninger, who had all been active in Catholic labour organisations. They strove to build up their own Resistance cells finding support in the Prelate and President of the Catholic labour organisations in Cologne, Otto Müller, and their Secretary General, Dr. Schmitt, who was later the Catholic student pastor in Berlin. Common ground with Goerdeler could easily be created and there is no reason to think that it was in any way more difficult to achieve close contact with Leuschner's circles, for the situation had greatly changed compared with the early years of the Opposition and with the state of mutual hostility that still prevailed among many of the *émigrés*. Within the trade union camp, at any rate, old frontier lines had lost their meaning; the battle against every form of totalitarian régime was the common aim of Catholic and Socialists as was the struggle for a responsible partnership of employees in State and industry. By the end of 1942, an organisational plan for a single trade union was ready in outline.

In the same front was Max Habermann, the former head of the German National Shop Assistants' Association, an organisation with right-wing tendencies. He was a personal friend of Goerdeler and lived occasionally in his house in Leipzig; he had contacts with remnants of his organisation. While the trade unionists and men of the labour organisations provided the Opposition with a network of functionaries some of whom may well have been the same men as those of the Social Democratic underground movement, and while they built up an organisation of contact men similar to that possessed by the Intelligence, the actual political impulses came from individual Socialist leaders. Several of them had already had close relations with Leuschner as a fellow-Hessian; the State Councillor Ludwig Schwamb, for instance, and particularly Dr. Carlo Mierendorff and Dr. Theodor Haubach. Mierendorff was generally accounted one of the most powerful and gifted opponents of the régime. He was not only an intellectual of great mental clarity, but a full-blooded personality and a born popular leader. He had suffered for more than four years in a concentration camp. After his release he joined forces with unbroken energy with his friend Dr. Theo Haubach, onetime publisher of the Socialist *Hamburger Echo*, who also had a long period of imprisonment behind him. Mierendorff was in touch with Canaris and was an important member of the Kreisau circle. According to Steltzer he confessed to one of the churchmen in this circle: "I have lived without religion. But I have come to the conviction that only Christianity can give meaning and significance to life." Haubach, too, belonged to this group of younger men who were inspired by religion. Turning inward, he "began to seek God in a new Christian fashion", as Gerstenmeier testifies.

Adolf Reichwein, who until 1933 had been professor at a teachers' academy, was also concerned with the questions of inner renewal. He particularly devoted himself to adult education and his strict Marxist principles did not prevent him living in the ideas of Grundtvig. At the same time it would be misleading to call these men right-wing Socialists. They may be called conservative in a cultural sense because the maintenance of creative, religious and artistic forces in the life of the people was a very serious aim with them. In social and political questions, on the other hand, they definitely belonged to the radical wing. All three typified in an exemplary manner this not unusual combination. It was a heavy loss for all oppositional groups when Mierendorff was killed in an air raid on Leipzig in December, 1943. Dr. Julius Leber succeeded him as the potential leader of the convinced Socialists. Four and a half years of brutal maltreatment by the SS had not managed to break his will; as a man to whom politics were a passion he was soon in the advance-guard of the conspiracy. Through Dahrendorf and Ernst von Harnack he came in contact with Goerdeler, but having an affinity for the military, he was closest to Trott and Stauffenberg. So the ranks were filled with those who were capable of assuming the reins of government as soon as the military coup took place and who had been selected for that task.

Preparations for that moment had been completed through the years and were very far reaching. No vacuum would have arisen if the Hitler régime had come to an end on 20th July and there would have been none of the embarrassing difficulties which arose after the capitulation in May, 1945. Naturally, there were differences of opinion among the political leaders. They concerned practical questions as well as the choice of personnel. Differences concerning the latter were at times very sharp and much can now be read about this in Goerdeler's biography. These tensions were combined with contrasting opinions concerning economic and politico-social questions to which we shall return. But in any case it was understandable enough that friction should be generated between personalities and characters under the heaviest spiritual pressure. The details do not concern us here; it will suffice to state the approximate results of discussions. In the course of the year 1943–44 agreement had been reached on a shadow government in which some of the positions were apparently interchangeable. Beck, at any rate, was to be the provisional

Head of State, Goerdeler Chancellor and Leuschner Vice-Chancellor with Jakob Kaiser as his deputy—this perhaps in case there should be a Republican form of government and Leuschner should stand for Reich President. Von Hassell was chosen for the Ministry of Foreign Affairs with von der Schulenburg as an alternative. For the post of War Minister Olbricht or Hoepner was named, with Stauffenberg as Under-Secretary of State. The important Ministry of the Interior (of decisive importance as it controlled the police) was to be taken over by Leber who was thus accorded a key position.

It is significant that a Socialist, Haubach, was also earmarked for the Propaganda Ministry if such was created. The Catholic labour leader Letterhaus was a candidate for the Ministry of Reconstruction. The list further included: Lejeune-Jung as Minister of Economics, Bolz (after Popitz had fallen out) as Minister of Culture and Dr. Wirmer as Minister of Justice. The Finance Ministry was to be headed by Loeser, a former mayor of Leipzig who had joined the Opposition as Managing Director of Krupp. Men of unexceptionable anti-Nazi character (such as Gessler, Steltzer and von Lüninck) were chosen for leading administrative posts in individual states and the larger towns.

At first sight this list of names may seem reminiscent of the artificial coalitions of the Weimar days—with a military "corset-bone" as its real support. But the differences compared with the pre-1933 period are clear. One of them consists in the fact that the men who now formed a coalition of so many different elements had come together under the pressure of highly unusual circumstances. None of them represented the average type of ambitious politician or was tied to an obsolete party programme. Moreover each one of them had to be prepared to stake his life for his convictions. All of them wore the "shirt of Nessus". In such a situation, other principles of selection apply than under the normal conditions of political life and real leaders are more likely to emerge in the process. Even so, one must not idealise the result. Hassell's talk of the "band of brothers" probably corresponded more to an imperative than to reality. This emerges clearly from Leuschner's last warning: "Be united!" The question of the contrast between the old ("the people of rank") and the young (the "activists"), between Conservatives and Radicals will have to concern us further. But whatever their practical differences of opinion, these men were united on a basis which, compared with the criminal régime which they sought to replace, recalls Goerdeler's "front of decency".

At any rate, the composition of the shadow government should make it easy to answer the question whether the conspiracy consisted of a group of anachronistic aristocrats, discontented generals and reactionary civilians who only came together or only began to show signs of life "when the war had been finally lost". But the political composition of the Opposition raises another question : to what extent did its leading members find an echo in the country? Were they broadly based? Were they in contact, not merely with loosely connected circles, but with the masses of the German people? Or did the Resistance operate in a kind of vacuum, doomed to misfire even if the military putsch succeeded?

In attempting to answer this question we must distinguish between two sets of facts : the first concerns the existence of a mass opposition in itself and the other, the presence of organic links between the "élite" and the broader oppositional movements.

A former German trade union leader, Paul, Maerker, who himself took an active part in underground work during the early years of the régime, estimates the number of workers organised in an anti-Nazi front at 125,000; that would be 3 per cent of the membership of the Free Trade Unions before 1933. He adds that 20th July took these groups completely by surprise : "No preparations had been made for co-operation with the Generals." But other evidence raises considerable doubts both as regards the numbers of organised opponents and the general suggestion that they lacked a plan. The idea still seems widespread that, as there were no headquarters with telephones and secretaries and no files of material have been found, there can have been no organisation or preparation of any kind. It is certainly correct that no prior warning was passed of the impending attempt on Hitler's life. But in the circumstances that was impossible. Not even the leading political personalities were informed of the details. But the existence of a network of cells can be taken as certain and the question is rather how far they were active in the conspiracy or whether they merely stood ready. Some general remarks have already been made on this subject when the new tactics of the Opposition after 1935 were discussed. For the later years there are more special sources of information. The statement may be thought too summary, but it had a certain symptomatic significance when a French worker in Germany reported in 1942 that in his factory "four or five men" belonged "to the organised Socialists". He believed the others were in sympathy with this cell. More convincing perhaps is the expressly stated "conservative estimate" made by the authors of the official American report on the effects of aerial bombardment. They write: "In the year 1944, one in approximately every 1,200 adults was arrested by the Gestapo for a political or religious offence. Organised opposition groups existed in most German towns." The report further states that oppositional activity was "normally confined, by necessity, to a local scale", but that the underground activity of trade unionists, Socialists and Communists was "on a national scale".

But some statements go much further and suggest a direct conspiratorial connection between the upper and the lower levels. Thus Alfred Weber felt justified in telling an American correspondent: "Thousands, literally thousands of civilians were involved in the assassination plot."

Much more detailed were the statements made by a German pastor at a meeting which we shall discuss later with the Bishop of Chichester in May, 1942. According to him trade union members had developed a network of go-betweens "during the last six months" which would allow them control of "key positions in big cities like Berlin, Hamburg and Cologne and over the whole country". The Social Democrat Emil Henk felt able to give even more complete details. He ascribed to Leuschner in particular the merit of having constructed an "invisible net" which covered the whole of Germany. He himself enumerated contact-men for certain parts of Baden and Hesse (from Heidelberg to Kassel) of whom each one, according to his statement, had to call on ten to twenty more anti-Nazis at the given moment. Henk's list of names mentions not only the inhabitants of large towns but of smaller communities down to villages. He estimates that in this one area alone ten to fifteen thousand anti-Nazis stood ready to act on 20th July.

Even if these statements—to which objections can be raised—were to be fully accepted, they would not indicate contact with really broad sections of the population. A mass organisation was simply out of the question. And as the military putsch failed, possible contact-men in small localities were not called upon. The orders given by the resisters in the War Ministry on 20th July were addressed only to "political representatives" and "liaison

G

officers" in the individual military districts. All the same, the statements under discussion cannot simply be dismissed and they contain a kernel of truth which alone should suffice to silence talk of the "rootless character" of the Opposition. Moreover, it can hardly be doubted that the mass of the silent Opposition, that broad reservoir of resistance under totalitarian rule, would in 1944 have risen at once and with fury against their oppressors once the coercive rule of the system had been broken.

Such an assumption is not contradicted by the fact that no spontaneous rising occurred when the Allies marched into the country in 1945. The psychological conditions were very different after a further year of aerial bombing, after an inconceivable accumulation of physical and moral destruction and in a situation which indeed implied "liberation", but at the same time conquest by the liberators.

If the existence of a broader revolutionary movement with mass support particularly of the left wing of the Coalition is taken as certain, admittedly other problems arise : Was there a more deeply founded political unity beside the community of moral convictions and beyond the negative goal of overthrowing Fascism and bringing the war to an end? Was there a community of ideas which could lead from the mere installation of a post-Hitler government to constructive action? Was there a reasonable prospect that the system of political and social democracy would take root? Or was the *coup d'état* foredoomed to be an episode (a Badoglio episode"), on account of the inner cleavage between "conservative" and "radical" tendencies or the "natural" dynamism of revolutionary movements?

These are questions of a speculative kind to which, of course, no final answer can be given. But evidence exists of the thought-content of the Opposition which is sufficiently significant to justify its discussion and which will lead us back beyond all practical considerations to its basic characteristics.

5. *Ideas on Constitutional and Social Reform*

Goerdeler, the tireless advocate of action, also concerned himself repeatedly and in very concrete detail with plans for the future. He set down more or less elaborate proclamations, programmes, memoranda and guiding principles which were based not in any way merely on ideas which he had thought up for himself. Discussions were held with Beck, Hassell, Jessen and Popitz, with members of the Churches and with the group of younger men who came together in the Kreisau circle. A continual exchange of views with Kaiser and Leuschner is also highly probable. Through the years Goerdeler wrote and improved on an "economic primer" which according to his widow came about as a result of conversations with trade union leaders and was intended to enable workers to take a stronger interest and a more active part in the management of "their" factory. It would introduce a false note into this study to call Goerdeler a "man of the people". But it is equally certain that he was socially minded in an honest and genuine sense. The spirit of the Bosch concern in which a conscious effort was made to give the workers a sense of partnership may have strengthened him in this.

It should further be mentioned that a number of writers and professors who were more or less close to the political Opposition shared in Goerdeler's plans. In particular, a group of political scientists, political economists and historians who taught at Freiburg University co-operated: Erich Wolf, Adolf Lampe, Constantin von Dietze, Walter Eucken and Gerhard Ritter. They belonged to the Confessing Church and it seems that Bonhoeffer put them in touch with Goerdeler. Here, too, was a basis for co-operation which extended beyond the purely political sphere. For social problems Professor Albrecht of Marburg was enlisted while in educational questions Professor Litt of Leipzig was Goerdeler's adviser.

The first formal programme we know of was still very sketchy. It was written in January–February, 1940, by Hassell who worked on it with Beck, Goerdeler and Popitz. It was to come into force if opposition to the attack in the West led to the hoped-for fall of the régime. It proposed a regency of three members who were to remain in power until "normal constitutional life" could be restored. The task of preparing for this moment fell to a nominated Constitutional Council. Meanwhile, executive power lay with the head of the Regency (Beck?) who delegated it to military district commanders. The declaration of a state of siege seemed inevitable if chaos was to be avoided and the "dignity of the law" restored. The programme specifically set this as the goal in sharp contrast to the moral devastation which had been the result of the preceding régime. The baneful consequences of Nazi rule and the first counter-measures to be taken were then briefly set out.

It seems that Goerdeler thought of putting the interim government at once on a popular basis. According to Hassell he planned
a plebiscite immediately after the fall of the régime.

As already mentioned, he believed in a rapid change of heart
as soon as truth was allowed to be spoken, "if only for twenty-
four hours". But his optimism was not shared by the other members of the circle. In additional drafts, Langbehn and Jessen
sketched a law on the state of siege which is said to have been very
drastic. Popitz also worked out a law "for the restoration of
orderly conditions in political and juridical life". His draft laid
great stress on the cleansing as well as on the efficiency of the
Civil Service. It was stated that the provisional order was to remain in force until "a permanent constitution can be introduced
with the co-operation of all classes of people in the German
Reich".

So far as the executive power was concerned, for some time
Goerdeler and his friends considered the restoration of the monarchy. They wished to found the highest authority on a "firm
central pillar" (Popitz), that was outside and above changing
opinions and party pressures. In view of experiences in the Hitler
period when the coupling of the two positions, that of party leader
and Head of State, had given the totalitarian system supreme power,
there was something to be said for a monarch at the apex. Gessler,
an old Democratic and South German Minister of the Weimar
Republic, favoured the restoration of the Wittelbachs. Just as
National Socialism originated in Austria and Bavaria, so the
legitimists had their strongest roots in South Germany. Presum-
ably the Bavarian members of the conspiracy would have preferred Crown Prince Rupprecht, the heir of the Wittelsbach line.
The heir to the Hohenzollerns, Crown Prince Wilhelm, was also
considered. According to Hassell, he declared himself "ready to
step into the breach and accept all sacrifices and dangers concerning which he had no illusions". But it is doubtful whether his
candidacy was considered as more than a transitional solution.
A more suitable candidate, at any rate, seemed to be Wilhelm's
second son, Louis Ferdinand. There were several points in his
favour : he could be considered a definite opponent of the Nazi
régime, he was in particular favour with Queen Mary, the British
Queen Mother, and he had worked for a time in the Ford factory
in the United States. An American business man with whom
Hassell was in contact felt able to assure him that on the other

side of the Atlantic Prince Louis Ferdinand would be "down-right popular".

There is reason to doubt whether this forecast was well-founded, even before the attack on Pearl Harbour. But it would be over-hasty to call the restoration of the monarchy an essentially undemocratic idea. The model visualised was evidently the British example of the monarch acting as president within a parliamentary system. And Goerdeler in particular was far from even desiring the restoration of the Prussian monarchy and its former power. Of the president, whether a monarch or a regent, he said specifically: "He is not intended to govern, but to watch over the constitution and represent the State." On a further point there was complete unanimity: the new régime was in no way to be reminiscent of the Kapp Putsch. This was a point of view urged by the military themselves and primarily by Hammerstein and Beck. The attitude of the younger generation in the Kreisau circle was even more energetic. In a conversation with Hassell, Trott zu Solz argued passionately that "internally and externally any semblance of reaction, 'gentlemen's club' or militarism must be avoided". This conversation of December, 1941, seems to have been decisive. As far as one can see, all talk of the monarchy vanished thereafter from the discussion.

Of greater interest than this isolated question are Goerdeler's plans for a constitution. They rested primarily on a high valuation of self-government. They therefore contained on the one hand a demand for decentralisation and a federalistic structure and on the other they proposed an electoral system designed to favour individuals who had already won their spurs in local or professional matters and had acquired a name with their electors. In all this Goerdeler intended to return to German traditions of a period when politics had not yet been collectivised, in other words, he proposed a "de-massing of the mass" (Ritter). To enable the Reichstag to take responsible action, Goerdeler suggested a restriction to three parties. For the same reason he desired to follow the British example of only personal candidates for election (instead of election by list) with decision in one ballot by simple majority. But only one half of the people's representatives were to be directly elected on the basis of universal suffrage; for the other half Goerdeler proposed indirect elections in stages starting from local representative bodies. Reichstag deputies had to be at least thirty-five years old and to have been

active for five years in local self-government. They also had to be
resident in the constituency for which they were a candidate. All
this clearly had the object of favouring practical experience and
local roots as against the strictly political elements. Further,
Goerdeler planned an upper house comprising representatives of
the larger occupational groups, employers' associations, the single
comprehensive trade union organisation and of the Churches and
universities. Apart from these vocational representatives, the free
co-option of fifty "notable Germans" of all classes was proposed.
To give the government greater stability, its fall could only be
procured in Goerdeler's plan by a qualified majority of the
Reichstag or by the agreement of both houses.

All this—which was mainly contained in a memorandum,
"The Goal", of 1941—did not represent any final plans and was
in no way an agreed programme of the Resistance movement.
But the preference for a conservative system of checks and balances is characteristic. There is some justification for saying that
Goerdeler harked back to the thoughts and work of Freiherr
vom Stein, though he did not share the latter's purely historical
preference for the propertied classes. There was no question of a
census. Apparently he wished to combine the original ideas of
Stein's municipal statutes with his own practical experience of
self-government in large communities. But the return to valuable
traditions is not synonymous with "reactionary romanticism".
We have Pechel's word that Goerdeler became increasingly open-
minded and indeed in many respects his thought reveals a considerable development. Jakob Kaiser, the Christian trade union
leader who survived the wave of executions and in Berlin after
1945 was to become one of the most stalwart defenders of democracy against the new threat from the East, said of Goerdeler
while he was still engaged in this battle that he would stand today
"on the side of the progressive forces of the people". Certainly,
a programme of widespread decentralisation including the dissolution of Prussia into its provinces and a federalistic structure
in general cannot be called "anachronistic".

Neither can other elements of Goerdeler's plans be hastily
labelled and so dismissed. They breathe a certain sobriety, one
might almost say an Anglo-Saxon sense for the concrete which
begins with the most practical necessities, with the radical reconstruction of a profoundly disrupted communal life. Granted such
an attitude, it seemed infinitely more important to be concerned

with the elementary content of political life and its efficient administration than with the trappings of party politics and mass demonstrations. In a conquered and partially destroyed Germany the revival of a more centralised and rationally constructed democracy of a kind which it had been attempted to introduce in 1919 was in any case bound to be an illusion. Moreover, Goerdeler and his colleagues knew very well that a simple return to the Weimar system was impossible also for other reasons. They wanted particularly to avoid the weaknesses in parliamentary structure that had contributed to the creation of a dictatorship (the continual change of government and the proliferation of parties) and they warned therefore against the electoral list system and proportional representation. These were certainly no obsolete ideas. The same applied to the desire for counter-poises to tendencies of irresponsible mass propaganda and demagogic leadership which, with subtle exploitation of these weapons, had proved so disastrous under a pseudo-legal régime.

Whether the means recommended to these ends, as for example the combination of direct and indirect representation and the stress laid on occupational representation, were adequate or were calculated to satisfy the genuine democratic needs of a people freed from tyranny is highly questionable. This was no more than a set of proposals of significance only for their general trend of thought. It was intended that they should be discussed by an advisory body, the *Reichsrat*, and this might have led to considerable changes. One thing at any rate is clear : within the "organic structure" of which Goerdeler spoke in one of his proclamations at the end of 1943 a considerable role was assigned to the trade unions and if their merger came about, their share might have been a decisive one. On the question of a united trade union, Goerdeler took up the ideas which had been worked out together by Leuschner, Kaiser and Habermann. They were entirely consistent with his own previous thoughts. Moreover it was a traditional line of trade union policy (as of communal policy) to value practical results and step-by-step progress above party doctrine, demagogic agitation or short cuts to the millennium. Here then a community of practical aims seems to have existed which might have offered a chance for political and social democracy to take root.

But a broader aspect must also be stressed. Goerdeler touched on it when he spoke of a "democracy of the Ten Commandments". Whatever the details of his constitutional plans, they centred on those religious and humanistic traditions and those inalienable values which underlie the conventional concepts of Western democracy. Thus it was stated in one of the numerous drafts of the radio speech which Goerdeler was to deliver after becoming Chancellor : "Through all the fog of propaganda the German people must learn the truth and nothing but the truth." The government, stated another sentence in the same document, would re-establish a State corresponding to the Christian tradition of the West based equally on the duty of its citizens and members to work in loyalty, self-sacrifice and service for the common good and on respect for the individual and his basic rights as a human being." It "begins its work by placing the power of the State under the laws of morality and justice.... All religious communities shall fulfil their divine task free of State supervision ... schools of all types shall be freed at once of the role so contrary to their purpose of serving to falsify facts, of offending young people's instinct for truth, of teaching them phrases instead of knowledge, hypocrisy instead of noble courage, brute strength instead of real ability.... Talented children from all classes of the people shall be admitted to all schools for which they are suited." The same. principles of "respect for truth" and "reverence for justice" infuse all the documents known to us. In a proclamation to the German people which Colonel-General Beck was to deliver, strong emphasis was laid on the moral degradation to which the previous régime had led, the blasphemous racial theory, the contemptible crimes, the soiling of German honour and the German name. No light promises were made. We shall have to struggle hard, it was stated, but we shall do so as "free men" and thereby recover "tranquillity of conscience". The most urgent task, declared another draft of the radio address, was the restoration of "the majesty of the law". Penance would have to be done for the persecution of the Jews and for crimes in occupied territories, and once again, in a final appeal, the task was set of "washing clean the German name so often dishonoured. We Germans alone can and will fulfil this task".

One could call this a programme of self-imposed "re-education" requiring a change of heart, repentance and a moral way of life. It lays more stress on a return to Christian and humanistic traditions than on outward requirements and formal patterns of behaviour. Its aim was to root out the National Socialist slave-morality, but not to implant a new one through propaganda and censorship. It imposed a task that could only be undertaken with a feeling of humility, with an awakened conscience and an awareness that in the last resort all men are sinners.

In the same context it may be of interest to inquire what plans the members of the shadow government had for the solution of another problem that was subsequently tackled so unfortunately —both in terminology and in practice—under the name "denazification". In one of their pronouncements they intended to say : "The sword of justice must strike without mercy those who degraded our Fatherland to the caricature of a State, who banished decency and the law, who allowed or fostered corruption and who enriched themselves while the mass of the people were impoverished.... Further, the responsibility must be determined by all those who in leading positions received and executed without protest orders which they knew to be contrary to law, to conscience and to the facts. Those too, must be called to account who outside Germany violated international law and the honour and dignity of honest human beings."

It can be argued that this is not a complete list of the crimes that were committed and that less tangible forms of the poisoning process which had continued for over ten years remain unmentioned. Here, too, Goerdeler adhered to his belief that there was only one front which mattered, that between the decent people and the "others" and that this dividing line was not determined by outward characteristics. Mere membership of a National Socialist organisation was therefore certainly not in itself a crime. Anonymous denunciations were to be ignored, false ones to be punishable, but everyone was called upon to inform the Minister of Justice of genuine crimes, whether of omission or commission. There was to be no hesitation regarding the real culprits, but there was little inclination to cast out mere camp-followers. The danger of being poisoned oneself in the battle against poison was fully realised, and of being tempted to adopt Hitlerian methods. If restoration of the majesty of the law was a main object of the new order, then a start could not be made by introducing retroactive laws. It seemed un-Christian to make a general call to revenge in which many shoddy motives might be involved. And it was obviously contrary to all the principles of civilised judicial procedure to assume that the accused was guilty if he could not prove himself innocent. The burden of proof lay, rather, with the prosecution. So far as can be judged on the basis of the proposed proclamations, the shadow government was determined to adhere to these basic elements of Western legal tradition.

In economic and social questions Goerdeler was in a special sense of the word more "western" than most of his friends of the older generation. It was one of his early and unshakeable convictions that free competition was a blessing. Economic life was to be disturbed as little as possible by the State and all bureaucratic governmental interference was to be avoided. His wishes therefore tended towards a restoration of free enterprise and free trade in so far as they were compatible with the common good, both in the national and the international sphere. While he stressed the rights of property, he showed no particular interest—at any rate in his surviving programmes—in the problem of large estates, and in the restriction of monopolies and combines only in the sense of the necessary control to maintain free competition. Only those *entrepreneurs* were to be expelled from business life who had "debased their economic responsibility and degraded themselves to become the spiritless tools of political bosses".

It was apparently this liberal creed of Goerdeler's which led to the clash between him and the younger generation, particularly the men from the Kreisau circle. Compared with his views, some of the older men—Popitz and Jessen, for instance, who supported a kind of planned economy and State Socialism—were closer to Moltke and his friends, though they did not share their position. As Beck did, thanks to his moral authority, they played the part of mediators. It was with reference to these differences and to other "restorationist" traits, but perhaps also to Goerdeler's inclination to return as soon as possible to parliamentary institutions that Hassell called him a "reactionary". That may seem surprising in view of Goerdeler's undoubted liberal convictions and coming from the pen of an aristocrat, and in the light of later experience it must be admitted that, after such a lengthy period of compulsory restriction followed by complete collapse, no economic recovery was possible without the release of personal initiative and individual profit motives. In the most literal sense of the word that would indeed be "reaction" against the Third Reich. But the question was—and still is today—whether the restoration of a Western system of a competitive society in the sense of mid-nineteenth century classical Liberalism or of a Neo-Liberalism was in keeping with the new social and the new international situation and whether Goerdeler's faith in a front of "decency" would have sufficed to restrain egotism. Only on the basis of such considerations which we shall meet in the Kreisau circle and which were particularly related to the social trends of a new century can the word "reactionary" have any serious meaning.

On the other hand, it would undoubtedly be very unjust to confuse Goerdeler's economic liberalism with social narrow-mindedness and reactionary class-consciousness. In municipal government he had co-operated closely with the trade unions. A memorandum which he wrote in prison gave the State the task of "making the workers share in bearing political responsibility". And in the economic parts of his programme he spoke of the active participation of employees in management and of the restoration of a just balance between classes through the organs of economic self-government. "The adjustment of wages", he stated, "shall as far as possible be secured through agreements freely negotiated between employers and trade unions supported by the State arbitration system whose value has been proved during recent decades." And he recommended the transfer "of the German social insurance system, which was once a model to the world, to the sphere of the workers' and employers' self-administration".

While there is every reason to stress the honesty of these views, one cannot and should not deny that, as already suggested, a dividing line opens here compared with another camp in the Resistance movement. It is certainly no accident that the word "restoration" or its concept occurs so often in Goerdeler's programmes. Restoration of the majesty of the law and of decent behaviour between men, restoration of inalienable human values, of human dignity, of freedom of thought and religion—all these were insistent demands. They rested on convictions which had been forged in the fire; they were shared by the "Right" and by the "Left" and so make these very terms meaningless. But the supporters of a "blitz" revolution from above wanted also to restore order as quickly as possible. That is, they wanted to avoid a real upheaval that might have included not only outbreaks of "lynch justice" and another "November", but also drastic social changes. That the Western powers would probably have the same aim after the occupation of Germany is not relevant to this hypothetical discussion. The essential point seems rather the programme of economic freedom and the restoration as far as possible of a predominantly bourgeois social order. Was there any basis for such a restoration and in so far as it existed was it not rapidly disintegrating? The trade unions which furthered the rise of the workers into the middle class might co-operate with Goerdeler, but would and could the Socialists follow the same line? And how would it be possible to fit the masses into such an order after they had been radicalised by oppression, had been impoverished and uprooted by air raids, evacuations and resettlement?

It can be argued and has, indeed, been argued that the fall of the Nazis was only the first step and that a second revolution would have to follow that of the élite. This possibility exists and it provides scope for more or less instructive speculation. But the suggestion that the Socialist members of the conspiracy, however many objections and claims they might raise, took part in it with mental reservations of this kind or that they planned to play the part of the armed men in the belly of the Trojan horse obviously mixes very false colours in the picture of events. One should certainly not attempt to gloss over the tensions which existed and the contrasts are well worth studying. But they should not be exaggerated or hardened in the sense of patterns or party catchwords of either the preceding or the following years. Just as the barriers between the Churches and trade unions of different kinds had been dropped, so points of contact and agreement arose between the other camps which belong or should belong to the heritage of the Resistance years.

Such a conception of the political character of the Opposition can be applied especially to the Kreisau circle as a kind of "leaven" which included in juxtaposition the strongest Conservative, Christian and Socialist elements without excluding the basic values of Liberalism, while the revolutionary or at least "radical" will of a younger generation of men gave it its particular colour. We now turn to a discussion of their ideas.

6. The Kreisau Circle

Since the summer of 1940 a group of men, mostly between thirty and forty had come together in a circle whose centre was Graf Helmuth J. von Moltke, the great-grand-nephew of the Field Marshal in the Bismarck era and the grandson of a Chief

Justice of the Union of South Africa. Before the war he had practised as a lawyer in Berlin and was also allowed to practise in England after he had passed the examinations there. To his friends from Oxford and London days he was known as an implacable anti-Nazi. During the war he served with the Combined General Staff as an expert on the rules of war and on international law : this position enabled him to protect a number of endangered persons, as others did in various ways. At the same time, he could provide military circles with legal weapons for use in combating some of the crass ideas in Hitler's conduct of the war.

The group whose centre he became took its name from his family estate of Kreisau, Silesia. Among its members were other aristocrats and bearers of old Prussian names. Nearest to Moltke was Graf Peter Yorck von Wartenburg who has already been mentioned as a cousin of Stauffenberg. He came from a family that had made a name in the military and political and also the intellectual history of Prussia. One of his ancestors was the general who began the war of liberation in 1812 by his act of "disobedience"; another has become known by his correspondence with the philosopher, Dilthey. Von Einsiedel and von Trotha, a cousin of Moltke's, belonged to this same aristocratic section of the group.

The participation of young East-Elbian aristocrats to a radical circle is not so surprising as may appear if the word "radical" is understood in its literal sense, that is, as a return to roots. Members of this group had taken part in the German youth movement of the 1920s which strove primarily for simplicity of life, purity of morals and a feeling of social responsibility and which was opposed to all empty social conventions. Sons of the Silesian nobility were to be found in the voluntary work-camps which brought together young people of all classes in an exchange of ideas and interests. With such experiences whose value was not weakened by the National Socialist distortion of these forms of communal life and with strong religious convictions they grew to manhood. They looked on their inheritance of large estates more as a responsibility than a privilege. They were prepared to consider the urgency of land reform objectively and without regard for their own interests, although they would certainly have opposed any form of "agrarian vandalism". In addition, there were certain specific insights and impulses which could be gained in the eastern provinces of post-Versailles Germany and which came to life at universities like Breslau and Königsberg. The basic questions which were discussed there in classrooms and seminars, at students' gatherings and in vacation time referred to a frontier-zone in which Germans and non-Germans were so intermingled and interlocked that the Western concept of the sovereign state and the nineteenth-century idea of the political nation paled to reactionary shadows. Supra-national and federalistic solutions were here most seriously discussed, a separation of nationality from politics for which the form of cultural autonomy offered itself. Standards of international morality were sought which would be binding on minorities on both sides of the frontiers. The whole stress of these efforts circled round the problem of peace between peoples as the only sound basis for peace between States. Fundamentally, the affirmation of a divine order was sought which would assure the dignity of the individual and the family, the dignity of all work, whether of the hand or the brain, and the dignity of every national community, so supplying an inner impetus to a new national and international society.

It is not surprising that radical Socialists could associate themselves closely with men of such basic views. We have already mentioned that Mierendorff, Haubach and Reichwein were active members of the Kreisau circle and that after Mierendorff's death, Leber took his place. The religious element linking the two wings was represented by four members of the group in particular, on the one hand by the Jesuit Father Delp, already mentioned, who was a priest in a suburb of Munich and influential among the Catholic youth, and by the provincial head of the Jesuits in Bavaria, Roesch, a man of importance for his well-balanced maturity of judgement. On the other hand, two members of the Confessing Church were active within the circle : Harald Poelchau, whom we have already met as prison chaplain in Tegel, and Eugen Gerstenmeier, a member of the External Affairs Office of the German Protestant Church who narrowly evaded death after 20th July. He had long been convinced that a purely spiritual opposition to National Socialism was not enough and that Nazism had to be rooted out if Christianity was to survive in Germany. During the war he was in charge of the spiritual welfare of foreign workers. This activity together with his participation in the Protestant Ecumenical movement gave him frequent opportunities for travel abroad. The strength of his religious conviction and his open-mindedness made him a particularly valuable member of the circle.

There were yet other men belonging to the group who could contribute to the common thought through their special experience or expert knowledge in particular fields : Paulus von Husen, a Westphalian Catholic, who had been a member of the "Mixed Commission" in Upper Silesia, as well as of the Supreme Administrative Court; Hans Lukaschek, a Catholic lawyer, formerly *Oberpräsident* of Upper Silesia, and Theodor Steltzer who after his removal from office as *Landrat* in Holstein had been active like Gerstenmeier in ecumenical work and as wartime transport officer in Norway had been able to prevent some projected acts of persecution. In 1945 he himself escaped death through his Norwegian friends who found a way of saving him from execution. The jurist Hans Peters from Breslau University also belonged to the Kreislau circle. Connection with Goerdeler was maintained through Fritz-Dietlof Graf von der Schulenburg (not to be confused with Friedrich Werner, the former Ambassador in Moscow), who as a robust and highly individual personality had the most varied contacts, but in essentials was in quite close accord with the Kreisau members. Contact with the oppositional group in the Foreign Office was secured by *Legionsrat* Hans-Bernd von Haeften and by Adam von Trott zu Solz. We shall have more to say of the latter in connection with his diplomatic activities. As a brilliant and dynamic personality he had a special place in the circle. Von Haeften was the son of a highly cultivated officer on the General Staff who had attracted attention in the first world war by a conflict with Ludendorff. Hans-Bernd, like his brother Werner, Stauffenberg's adjutant, was deeply rooted in the Evangelical faith, but also in the conviction that even a Church that did not possess a binding social doctrine had an obligation to offer Christian advice in worldly matters. The firmness of his character and the sensitiveness of his conscience are stressed by his Kreisau friends. In close contact with Moltke and his circle and particularly active was also Graf von Schwerin-Schwarenfeld who through close relations with Oster and Dohnanyi and also as Witzleben's assistant adjutant had belonged to the circle of the conspiracy at an early stage. Through him and the younger Graf Schulenburg (and also through Yorck and Stauffenberg) the threads ran to the military Resistance movement.

This was the group of men who used to foregather, though not always in full numbers, as often as opportunity arose and who tried to work out certain programme-points. In particular, three meetings attended by a large number of members took place in Kreisau. Each lasted several days, one in the spring, another in the autumn of 1942 and the third in the spring of the following year. Moltke's own view of the situation at this time appears in a letter which he sent to a British friend (Lionel Curtis) in the middle of the war in 1942. In it he spoke of the continual danger in which they lived and of the release of the "beast in man". But he also mentioned hopeful symptoms of which the most important, he said, was "a religious awakening that has started and that is accompanied by a readiness if need be for death". While Moltke and his friends were themselves witness to such a movement, he confirms the view (which has been variously expressed in this study) that a renewal of the spirit and a return to convictions of a basic kind were being heralded in those sections of the German people who had consciously been "through the fire". Moltke found that not only were the Churches in general increasing in influence but that the young generation were undergoing a change. "Today", he wrote, "not a numerous, but an active part of the German people are beginning to realise, not that they have been led astray, not that bad times await them, not that the war may end in defeat, but that what is happening is sin and that they are personally responsible for each terrible deed that has been committed—naturally, not in the earthly sense, but as Christians."

In view of such a situation, Moltke and his friends saw it as their task to "visualise Europe after the war". The letter continues : "We can only expect to persuade our people to overthrow this régime of terror and frightfulness if we are able to point to a goal beyond the paralysing and hopeless immediate future.... For us, Europe after the war is less a problem of frontiers and soldiers, of top-heavy organisations and grandiose planning. The real question which will face postwar Europe is how the picture of man can be restored in the hearts of our fellow-citizens. But this is a question of religion and education, of the organic connection between occupation and family, of the proper relationship between responsibility and rights." He adds that he and his friends felt considerably encouraged by contact with "Christian groups in the various occupied territories". Only in

France, he believed, was there "occasional action, but as yet no opposition of a really basic character".

This attitude which seems to lay more stress on fundamental concepts than on deeds has been compared to Gandhi's "non-resistance". There are indeed points of contact, but such a parallel requires considerable qualification. We may note here that Moltke himself spoke in his letter of persuading the people to "overthrow the government" by offering them a worthwhile goal. But it is true that the main purpose of the Kreisau circle was not conspiratorial activity and the preparation of a Putsch. Moltke and his friends wanted rather to create the basis for a post-National Socialist Germany and a post-National Socialist Europe in both of which the false Nazi gods should have been rooted out through bitterest experience. No uprising could in itself, of course, heal the deep-seated evil. Moltke inclined rather to the view that it would have to run its full course and that an internal revolt would only confuse the issues. Indeed, to a certain extent he kept aloof from the activists. But this needs more precise interpretation and we must therefore now turn to the ideas of the Kreisau circle.

The main ideas on which the members of the group were agreed are set forth in a number of documents of which five have been preserved. Some of them are dated May, 1942, and August, 1943. Again, as in the case of Goerdeler, there are no definitive programmes. Later versions have been lost and modifying additions were contemplated. But the main points are laid down with all the clarity that could be desired. Firstly, the basic view is stressed that reconstruction must be based on "freedom-loving labour" and on the Christian Churches. It would be a grave misunderstanding to assume that this represented a tactical compromise, a concession to the Socialists in order to win them over to an acceptance of Christian principles. All were agreed that the totalitarian claim of the State could only be overcome by an equally totalitarian spiritual claim, that is, by submission to ultimate and unqualified demands. Graf Peter Yorck expressed this antithesis with the utmost resolution and logical clarity when he declared at his trial before the People's Court: "The essential is the totalitarian claim of the State on the citizen with disregard for his religious and moral obligations before God." And the presiding judge in Moltke's trial, the infamous Freisler, indirectly and unconsciously recognised where the kernel lay in the convictions of the Kreisau circle when he said: "Only in one respect

H

does National Socialism resemble Christianity : we demand the whole man."

As regards the basic attitude of the circle it is not without interest that Moltke's thoughts only gradually reached this extreme point of contrast. In the letter to his British friend from which we have quoted sentences he says that before the war he had assumed that a belief in God was not essential for an enemy of the régime. He now knew, he added, that this was "wrong, completely wrong" and that purely moral principles did not suffice to enable men to risk all and sacrifice all.

Whatever one's own attitude to such a statement, Tresckow or Lehndorff, Beck or Hermann Kaiser, Hammerstein or von Kleist and probably thousands of unknown people could have said the same. And the attitude of some of the radicals among the Socialists was no different, as Steltzer specifically says of Mierendorff. Personal experience must have brought them in close contact with the source of strength whose effect was so apparent among the conservative radicals. That they overstepped the bounds of Marxist orthodoxy or of indifferent free thought can hardly be doubted. Otherwise it would be unthinkable that their jointly agreed principles should lay so strong an emphasis on the "divine order" as the "criterion of relations between men and peoples" and as the binding force which alone could overcome the anarchy "of a power structure based exclusively on technological supremacy". The "principles" therefore particularly stressed complete freedom of conscience, the dignity of the individual, protection of family life and an organic development of communal life. State schools were to be "Christian Schools" with religious instruction of both Confessions as an obligatory subject, and this instruction was as far as possible to be given by churchmen themselves.

The further suggestions made by the Kreisau circle in regard to education cannot be discussed here, although they are of interest for many still very topical problems. New school books were called for and the withdrawal of the old ones, even if no substitute was yet available. At the same time, however, Moltke and his friends were emphatic opponents of all mere pragmatism and behaviourism. They insisted on preserving the classical tradition of the German *Gymnasium* and on the separation of professional schools from the universities; the latter were to be seats of research and teaching with a universal frame of reference and in the combination of living quarters with place of work were to stress communal life—and in this Moltke was clearly thinking of the English college system. The relationship between the State and the Churches was to be regulated by free contracts. Eventually it was hoped to achieve a "German community of Christians" to which all believers would belong irrespective of their Confessions.

A very concrete application of Christian ethics and of the conviction of the "dignity of man" can be seen in the economic part of the programme, and here the progressive element of thought emerges most distinctly. The Kreisau circle supported an "ordered system of competitive production" combined with a high degree of economic self-government. In this programme were included : a "disentanglement" of monopolistic cartels and combines for the sake of general interests, a land reform, the nationalisation of mines and key industries, the development of co-operative organisations between employers and employees with the participation of the latter in management and in "the products of industry, particularly increment value". It was further intended to set up a single "German trade union" such as was also planned by Goerdeler, Kaiser and Leuschner. But it appears that the Kreisau circle intended this organisation to assume only the "higher direction" until the tasks undertaken by it could be entrusted to the State and the self-governing organs of industry, trade, crafts and agriculture. The principle was stressed throughout that the natural sources of wealth should serve the common good and that the influence as well as the responsibility of the German workers should be increased.

While the strong admixture of Socialist elements in organisational and practical economic questions gave the Kreisau plans a position "between East and West" which will be discussed in another context, the legal thinking of the circle, as everything which concerned the "personal" sphere, had an entirely Western orientation. In fact, the two drafts dealing with the punishment of "the desecrators of law" are among the most impressive expressions of the idea of the *Rechtsstaat* which has grown up in the centuries of modern history and is to be considered as the cornerstone of civilisation. The desecration of divine and natural as well as of statutory law was to be punished. The proposals in this connection went considerably further than those made by Goerdeler. In certain cases they included proceedings before the Hague Court of Justice, in other words they counted on a system of international penal justice. But the stress which was laid here on the "majesty of the law" was not so different from Goerdeler's demand.

The drafts then carefully discussed the problem of "retroactive legislation" and the principle of *nulla poena sine lege*, stating that historically this principle was to be understood as a barrier to absolute and arbitrary power and though it did not correspond to any basic requirement and moreover had been most seriously infringed by the malefactors in question, yet the return to security under the law and the revival of confidence in the law required its definite retention. As a solution to this dilemma it was suggested that, in cases of "adequately suspected persons", the courts could issue a "statement declaring a violation of the law" even in retrospective cases, but that punishments could only be imposed if the offence came under laws existing at the time of the deed. Such a "declaratory statement" could entail acts of atonement, but was principally intended to revive a sense of justice and to create a precedent for the future. The statement of the penal court might also be accompanied by reparation orders and administrative measures in the field of civil or political rights. While it was desired to avoid in this way the danger of lawless arbitrariness and the undiscriminating pursuit of revenge, the circle considered that most of the National Socialist crimes—including complicity and the execution of orders of a criminal nature—came in any case under existing laws and could therefore be punished by normal legal procedure. The suggestions concerning international crimes are of no less interest. They underlined with maximum force the necessity of a legally ordered community of peoples. But for the sake of this very ideal a morally acceptable solution had to be found which was not the victors' revenge, but which represented with all clarity a "triumph of law" and a "cornerstone" of peace. The demand of the nations for punishment was undeniably justified. But punishment by organs of the victorious powers would have a destructive effect on law. The relevant draft therefore suggested that the International Court of Justice at the Hague should be accorded the same competence to issue declaratory statements in regard to desecrators of the law as it was intended to grant German courts. Enough cases of crime would remain which could be punished on the basis of statutory law, either international law or the law of the countries concerned. In such proceedings six judges were to sit of which three should be drawn from the victorious powers, two from neutral countries and one from the conquered state. The indictment was a matter for that nation whose laws had been violated; execution of sentence, however, was not to lie in its hands, but was to be carried out by the court of another country. Once more the warning was underlined that an advance in the morality of international relations could only be achieved if the sovereignty of the law was recognised, but not if force was answered with force.

Two other drafts of the Kreisau circle are concerned with the political reconstruction of Germany. While in his letter to his British friend in 1942 Moltke acknowledged and foresaw with not unjustifiable pessimism that their fight might come to an end with Germany's "total collapse as a national unit", his practical suggestions were made in the hope of being able to set up a federative whole—first in Germany and then in Europe. Instructions were laid down for "provincial administrators" who were to take over the government after the fall or collapse of the régime. In place of the old historical states, provinces (*Länder*) were to be set up, each with a population of 3–5 millions and with boundaries corresponding roughly to those of the military districts. The principal tasks of the administrators would be to ensure food supplies, to purge the apparatus of local government and in co-operation with the trade unions and the Churches to start on the restoration of law and decency as well as the most necessary reforms in the administrative and economic system.

Beyond these first emergency measures, a programme of reconstruction was expounded in a detailed memorandum. First, it stressed those basic religious and social demands which have already been discussed. Then the draft sketched the structure of the German Reich which was to be in harmony with the natural articulation of human life in the family, the local community and in "balanced economic areas". Political responsibility was first to be developed in small circles, that is, by responsible participation in recognisable neighbourly units and within the framework of tasks with which the man in the street was familiar. Accordingly, only local and district representatives were to be elected directly. Every citizen over the age of twenty-one was entitled to vote, but the memorandum planned to give heads of families an additional vote for each child below that age. Eligibility for election was confined to a minimum age of twenty-seven. Political officials and members of the armed forces were not eligible. Local and district councils would then elect the provincial assemblies and these the Reichstag. At least one half of those elected were not to come from these electing bodies. Finally, the provincial diet elected the provincial commissioner and the Reichstag the Reich President, both with a term of office of twelve years. The Reich Chancellor formed his own cabinet; he was to be appointed by the President with the approval of the Reichstag which could vote him from office with a qualified majority provided he suggested a successor. Here the idea of a "constructive vote of no confidence" which was implicit also in Goerdeler's thought is clearly expressed. In addition, a Reich Council was to be formed comprising the provincial commissioners, the President of the Reichstag, the chairman of the chambers of commerce and members appointed by the Reich President. The upper house was intended to be an advisory body, but was also to have disciplinary jurisdiction over the Reich government and the provincial governments.

It has seemed necessary to convey the basic essentials of these proposals because they reveal the similarities with and contrasts to the plans of other groups and particularly of Goerdeler's who recorded his ideas so much more systematically, completely and rationally. Compared with his ideas one could be tempted to call those of the Kreisau circle obscure, romantic or unpolitical. But just as the plans of the Leipzig Oberburgermaster and his administrative experience do not fit into the scheme of practical politics with their moral assumptions and their content of optimistic faith and this has therefore been stressed by Goerdeler's biographer as an illusory element, so it appears mistaken to dismiss as crude dilettantism the ideas of the Kreisau circle which were based on a different *Weltanschauung* but also on "experience". In contrast to faith in the infallibility of reason there was expressed here the much less optimistic conviction of the necessity of a new "basis of order" in a world devastated by demonic powers and repeatedly exposed to them. In this dimension the contrast indeed goes very deep; its political effects continue into our own time and it certainly is not synonymous with the contrast between old and young and quite certainly not between people of rank and activists.

The effect of this contrast is therefore of considerable interest. It is indicated by a number of statements and references. The most important and from a source point of view the best assured evidence occurs in a letter in which Dr. Gerstenmaier describes a conference of December, 1942, or January, 1943. He states expressly that "this great discussion which had been prepared for weeks beforehand was one of the most interesting events in the preparation of the *coup d'état*". He further notes that the difference was "not really" that between young and old, but one between the younger group and Goerdeler, also that the basic divergence came to light in social and economic questions. Those taking part in the conference were Beck, Goerdeler, Popitz, Hassell, Jessen as well as the nucleus of the Kreisau circle. Beck, states the letter, was merely a listener, while Popitz and Hassell (and, from the other side, the younger Schulenburg) acted as intermediaries, Moltke became "very polemical" and finally— Haubach and Mierendorff having been prevented from attending for "political reasons"—Gerstenmaier undertook to draw a "sharp antithesis" between the economic and social ideas of the Kreisau circle and those of Goerdeler.

This evidence—which has been overlooked in most discussions —confirms what can likewise be deduced from a comparison of the relevant sections in the programmes. Basically, like so many men who came from the New Conservatives or the youth movement of the 1920s, the leading members of the Kreisau circle had broken with the bourgeois pattern of thought. They had outgrown most of the "liberal" articles of faith of the nineteenth century and the social and economic concepts of the Weimar Republic. Thus far they were certainly at a greater distance from Goerdeler than from Popitz and Hassell and yet at the same time they stood on their own ground. On the other hand it must not be overlooked that the common Christian convictions formed a strong link, particularly with Goerdeler, neither was the former mayor of Königsberg unacquainted with the intellectual tendencies which were so widespread among political personalities in the East. For him no less than for Moltke the restoration of human dignity was a question of "religion and education, of the organic connection between occupation and family, of the proper relationship between responsibility and rights". In fact, when one goes into details of the comparison, beside the differences a considerable area of common ground is revealed. Despite the contrast, this applies even in economic and social matters in so far as Goerdeler laid strong emphasis on the influence and responsibility of the working population. It is altogether possible that between 1942 and 1944 the Kreisau circle exerted increasing influence in this direction and penetrated Goerdeler's thought with its own.

Political differences were from the beginning less distinct. The Kreisau circle, including its Socialist members, opposed no less than Goerdeler both a uniform and formal democratic structure and the French concept of the "one and indivisible nation" or the dogma of the sovereignty of the people. On both sides they were much more convinced of the value of a "democracy of the grass-roots" and of the necessity of building up from below. Indeed, Goerdeler went considerably further than the Kreisau circle in the application of the principle of direct popular elections, but he went considerably less far than they in the question of decentralis-ation, let alone in wanting to create new provinces. Nevertheless, he, too, contemplated the dissolution of Prussia, though not so much under the moral and political aspect as the Kreisau mem-bers. But on the whole these parts of his programme show no tendencies which are in complete contrast to the ideas of the Kreisau circle or which excluded contact with it. Leber, the strongest figure among the Socialists, is said to have found Goer-deler's programme "not constructive enough", but he believed he could achieve his aims as Minister of the Interior in Goerdeler's cabinet. And it is significant that among initiates in the last stage there was talk of a Leber-Goerdeler-Stauffenberg trio.

In view of all this there is little reason to overstress the contrast between revolutionary and restorationist tendencies or to speculate on the necessity of a break. Particularly those who believe that the differences touched on fundamental questions will find the measure of agreement surprisingly great. After its fashion the Kreisau circle also aimed at "restoration", that is, at the re-estab-lishment of the "picture of man". In this re-education Moltke and his friends saw a prime prerequisite of democracy. In prac-tice that was not so far removed from Goerdeler's "democracy of the Ten Commandments". In exactly the same way as Goerdeler they provided for conservative counterpoises, for instance by raising the age of eligibility for election or by restricting those irresponsible mass impulses which had contributed so much to the rise of Hitler. The revolutionary energy of the Kreisau circle was not directed to "grandiose planning" for a new order of society; it was radical in its demand for a break with the materialistic past and a revival of those moral forces in which Goerdeler also believed. Its most immediate and direct contribution to the Resistance movement therefore appears as a fermentative element that worked from within rather than from without; admittedly, the ideas which the Kreisau members put forward went beyond that, but they should not be underestimated or discredited as "mystic" because of the fact that in decisive matters they still represent a challenge.

But there was another difference between Goerdeler and the Kreisau members which, beside other evidence, Gräfin Moltke has touched on with the statement that her husband and his friends never agreed with Goerdeler's plans for action, and despite their respect for him personally, "would have nothing to do with his dubious methods of conspiracy". Primarily this objection was not religiously or philosophically, but politically motivated and was directed against lack of caution, against lists of ministers and continual debate. But a "Gandhi element" also played a part in it and as an opposite position this requires clarification if a very considerable aspect of the German Opposition is not to be mis-interpreted. In truth not one of the main participants in the conspiracy had been spared the agonising question whether force was permissible or could represent a cure of any kind. None of them belonged to the adventure-seeking or asocial type whom resistance attracted as such. Yet they answered the question in the affirmative under the impulse of that categorical demand which has been most clearly formulated by Tresckow: it was all impor-tant "for the German Resistance movement to have risked its life on daring the decisive throw before the world and before history". It can be proved that among the Kreisau circle Gerstenmaier shared this belief from the point of view of the clergyman and his responsibility: religious resistance was not enough. His letter pre-viously mentioned gives explicit evidence of this. He not only calls the discussion between the older and the younger generation in January, 1943, "one of the most interesting events in the pre-paration of the *coup d'état*", but ends with the statement that all participants, including Moltke, were agreed on the necessity of "carrying out the *coup d'état* as quickly as possible".

In fact, members of the Kreisau circle, for instance Yorck, took an active part in the preparations and Gerstenmaier was arrested by the Gestapo at the headquarters of the revolt on 20th July. The assumption that, if he had been at liberty, Moltke would have done everything to prevent the attempt on Hitler's life is not unfounded. But he would certainly not have diverged from his friends on this point. The dividing line between thought and action, which did indeed exist, was not so clear cut. As the Gräfin Moltke herself says in one of her comments, the Kreisau circle did not exclude "the application of force". Admittedly, the members saw it as their special task to fill the spiritual and political vacuum which they believed would follow the war and the collapse of the régime—whether or not the latter continued its course to the end or was overthrown. That this basic standpoint emerged with such clarity was in Moltke's own opinion the work of God and not of men.

This interpretation is confirmed by two very unusual letters which Moltke wrote to his wife in January, 1945, from prison in Tegel. In one of them he notes almost with rejoicing that he was to die for precisely those things for which he was really responsible, not for actions of any kind or conspiracies, but for his thoughts. He paid tribute to the political insight of Freisler, the brutal president of the People's Court, for having set him apart from all political activity and from the Goerdeler group. "Thus it is documented", states the letter in conclusion, "that not plans, not preparations, but the spirit as such shall be persecuted. *Vivat Freisler!*"

No historian will wish to comment on these words. They are a testimony whose full weight should work upon the reader. But Moltke himself added an interpretation. In a second letter he praised God who had so wonderfully prepared "his unworthy vessel" : "At the very moment when I was in danger of being drawn into active putsch preparations—Stauffenberg visited Peter (Yorck) on the evening of the 19th (January, 1944)—I was removed so that I was and remain free of any connection with the use of force." Thus in his eyes it was a higher dispensation which "removed him" through his arrest six months before the attempt on Hitler's life in order to bring the meaning of his life to completion. And so there was no talk at his trial, as Moltke wrote, of a "tortuous character" or "complicated thoughts" or "ideology". Once again he praised the merciful dispensation of God which had separated him from all class interests and all patriotic motives so that he could testify to the deepest force of the Resistance. He stood before Freisler, states another pregnant sentence, "not as a Protestant, not as a great landowner, not as an aristocrat, not as a Prussian, not as a German ... but as a Christian and as nothing else".

Beside this fundamental interpretation of the part played in events by the Kreisau circle and its principal members, there remains only one more minor and purely factual question to discuss. Did not those who themselves were further removed from the deed indirectly put pressure on the conspirators and so, perhaps prematurely, help to precipitate the attempt? Moltke was arrested in January, 1944, for having warned Consul General Kiep that the Gestapo were looking for him. Then on 22nd June, Leber and Reichwein made contact with the central committee of the Communist underground movement. This attempt to widen the front or to insure against a stab in the back in the event of a general rising had, it is presumed, fateful consequences. It put the Gestapo, which had infiltrated into the Communist ranks, on to the right track. A few days later, Leber and Reichwein were arrested. The opinion has been expressed that, in view of this fact, Stauffenberg was obliged to act, come what might, in order to save his friends and prevent the full disclosure of the plot. But if one recalls that repeated attempts had been made on Hitler's life since February, 1943, and by Stauffenberg himself since December, 1943, such a thesis does not seem to have much weight.

But the contact with the Communists raises a much more important question. Does it reveal evidence of a basically "Eastern" orientation of the Kreisau circle (and of Stauffenberg) compared with the "Western" orientation of Goerdeler and his friends? Did, as Gisevius has attempted to convince his readers, a "militant Socialism" of the younger members (principally Leber and Schulenberg) or Stauffenberg's "militaristic" influence intend to deflect the stream heading for catastrophe into the river-bed of a national Bolshevism? Was Stauffenberg a "Super-Prussian", a "soldier through and through", to whom "salvation of the Fatherland" and "salvation of the *Wehrmacht*" were synonymous? The answer must be that this interpretation is radically false and that it would be hard to show a deeper misunderstanding of the main motive which Stauffenberg had in common with the Kreisau circle, that is of his fundamental rejection of every totalitarian system, whatever its political or social colour might be. It must also be said that this misinterpretation is not confined to writers of memoirs—where the background of resentment and overcompensation is clear enough—but that it has also had an effect on historical reality in that it aroused the impression in the American intelligence service (via statements made to A. W. Dulles) that

Stauffenberg was playing with the idea of a "revolution of workers, peasants and soldiers", that he hoped for a Communist Germany, organised after the Russian pattern and supported by the Red Army. On the contrary, it can be stated here that, like the other men of the Kreisau circle, Stauffenberg lived rather in a universal than a military or nationalistic perspective. His thoughts and plans were directed to the liberation of all peoples living under a tyrannical régime, and certainly not to the replacement of Hitler's dictatorship by one of Stalin.

A closer discussion of the important East-West problem will be given in the next chapter, which deals with the German Opposition as a part of the great international struggle. The picture of the Opposition would be incomplete without an examination of its aspects in foreign policy; indeed, the attempt to reach a comprehensive judgement will depend in part on whether and to what extent the German oppositional elements strove to restore peace, on the direction taken by their thoughts on the future of Europe and on the attitude shown by the Allies towards them.

THE OPPOSITION AND THE ALLIES

1. Peace Feelers

THE existence of a German Opposition to Hitler was officially passed over in silence abroad and later misinterpreted but was nevertheless well known. In particular, leading statesmen of the West cannot well have been uninformed on important details. They received the "green reports" and other information from Germany which gave a more or less accurate picture of the Socialist and Communist underground movement. They were further informed and approached directly by a number of Germans who were actively involved in the conspiracy, men in private as well as in official positions, soldiers as well as civilians. They received offers of co-operation and joint resistance at a time when it would still perhaps have been possible to prevent the war and put an end to the nightmare with which a régime of criminals threatened not only Germany, but large parts of Europe.

It has been shown that the British Foreign Secretary and Prime Minister in particular were completely conversant with the attitude and plans of the German Opposition in the summer and autumn of 1938. The same applies to their Conservative critic, Winston Churchill, and he even revealed his knowledge publicly. In one of his inflammatory speeches Hitler had maintained that if Churchill and his friends were in power they would work directly for war with Germany. In a speech broadcast to the U.S.A. on 17th October Churchill replied that the contrary was true. If he or Anthony Eden or Duff Cooper were Prime Minister they would have built up a powerful security system to deter the German dictator from war. And he added: "This would have been an opportunity for all peace-loving and moderate forces in Germany, together with the chiefs of the German Army, to make a great effort to re-establish something like sane and civilised conditions in their own country."

Thus in a manner which was hard to justify Churchill revealed knowledge based on highly confidential communications made in this case particularly by von Kleist. The German Opposition had repeatedly been obliged to warn against such indiscretions, even of the most well-meaning kind. Naturally, Hitler did not allow this reference to internal German opposition to escape him and in a statement to the Press on 7th November Churchill felt called on to assuage the incensed dictator's anger. It was deliberately and in this connection that he made the oft-quoted statement: "I have always said that if Great Britain were defeated in war I hoped we should find a Hitler to lead us back to our rightful position among the nations. I am sorry, however, that he has not been mellowed by the great success that has attended him." These words were not calculated to appeal to the German Opposition which certainly reproached Hitler with more than lack of "maturity"; but apparently Churchill wished to make good his indiscretion and talk the Führer out of his suspicion. So he continued: "Herr Hitler showed himself unduly sensitive about suggestions that there may be other opinions in Germany besides his own. It would be indeed astonishing if, among 80,000,000 of people so varying in origin, creed, interest and condition, there should be only one pattern of thought. It would not be natural; it is incredible."

It cannot be said that efforts were lacking on the German side to strengthen the view that there was in fact more than "one pattern of thought" among the citizens of the Third Reich. In particular, Goerdeler's journeys abroad in 1937–38 should be remembered when he certainly made energetic attempts at enlightenment. In December, 1938, he sent his foreign friends a "world peace programme". In this he urged the calling of a preliminary conference of the Powers which amongst other things should concern itself with the stabilisation of currencies, the working out of a generally recognised international "moral code" and progressive disarmament. The last sentence of the programme stated: "Whoever abstains from co-operating wants war and is a breaker of the peace." In May of the following year (1939) Goerdeler once again visited England and France. He also had a conversation with Churchill and probably with Vansittart. Similarly, Schlabrendorff was received by Lord Lloyd and Churchill, and Pechel states he was in London three times in the spring of 1939. We have already mentioned Trott's mission in the summer and the activities of the brothers Kordt shortly before the pact with Russia.

With the outbreak of war the possibility of such contacts naturally became more limited and their purpose was bound to change. Weizsäcker arranged that Theo Kordt should be assigned to the Legation in Berne in order to maintain contact with London from there. When hostilities started and began to spread, a main object of the German Opposition was to prevent the difference between the German Government and the German people from becoming effaced and the programme of a punitive peace from creating the "monolithic" compactness of which Goebbels was always talking. Indeed, in one of his early war speeches Neville Chamberlain laid strong emphasis on the fact that the "German Government" was the obstacle to peace and denied any "vindictive purpose". This statement was also passed by letter through an intermediary to Kordt and was interpreted by him—in fact, mistakenly—as a promise of a direct kind to the Opposition and in that sense handed on to the military as a means of encouragement.

This leads to the phase of plans for an uprising between the Polish and French campaigns which has already been dealt with in the section on the "Military Sector". As we have indicated, the aim of the foreign contacts at this time was to obtain assurance of a reasonable peace and then of a suspension of military operations so German weakness following on a military putsch should not be exploited by the opponents in the West. For this purpose several actions were started. Goerdeler made soundings through Stockholm and the King of the Belgians. It also appears that the former Reich Chancellor Joseph Wirth opened up a channel of communication from Switzerland to England. Some kind of offer does in fact seem to have been made by the British; it was passed on by the former Reich Defence Minister Gessler, but never reached the Germany Army chiefs. But the main approach took place through the Vatican and the British Minister there, Mr. Osborne. It was undertaken by the Munich lawyer, Dr. Joseph Müller, who was among the conspirators in the Intelligence and was at the same time an emissary of Cardinal Faulhaber, the Archbishop of Munich.

Details of the negotiations and their result do not concern us here. It was recorded in the controversial "X-report" and hardly contained such far-reaching assurances—on, for instance, German frontier questions—as were passed on by Dohnanyi as a "stimulant".

Hassell's activity and its negative result emerge more clearly. On 22nd–23rd February, 1940, and again on 15th April, he met the Englishman, Lonsdale Bryans, in Arosa. The latter had offered himself for this mission to the British Foreign Secretary, Lord Halifax, on the strength of a connection with Hassell's Italian son-in-law. In their first discussion Hassell stressed that the upheaval must be a matter for the Germans and then concentrated on a peace programme which he wrote out for transmission to Halifax. Apart from general principles of peaceful reconstruction and the restoration of Poland and Czechoslovakia, Hassell's proposal was that Austria and the Sudetenland should remain with the Reich and that the German-Polish frontier should resume its 1914 form. But the British intermediary now found no further hearing in the Foreign Office and he was merely allowed to meet Hassell once again for the purpose of breaking off relations.

Hassell was not exactly successful in his other efforts, either. In the first year of war he was in close contact with the American *Chargé d'Affaires* in Berlin, Alexander Kirk. When Sumner Welles, the Under-Secretary in the State Department, came to Berlin in February, 1940, Hassell tried to persuade Kirk to put him in contact with other than only "official people". He suggested Popitz and Planck. But apart from a conversation between Sumner Welles and Schacht, there were no private talks. On the contrary, the American visit had an unintended pro-Nazi effect. Much to the disappointment of the Opposition, it appeared to enhance Hitler's prestige as a possible partner in peace negotiations. In vain Goerdeler suggested that Sumner Welles should not go straight from Rome to Berlin, but should visit Paris and London first, where he would be so "enlightened" that he would abandon the last stop in his journey.

These are a few sidelights only on the relations of the Opposition with the Western Allies. Neutral countries such as Spain, Portugal and Turkey offered further points of contact. Among those who co-operated with Hassell in exploiting these opportunities Albrecht Haushofer may be mentioned, the son of the geopolitician, who after a severe inner struggle had become a resolute opponent of the régime. That it was not only the disastrous Nazi foreign policy which determined his attitude, or at any rate that he far outgrew a merely technical opposition is revealed in his "Moabit sonnets" which are among the most impressive moral and religious documents of the German Resistance movement.

Finally, the activity of Goerdeler must once more be recalled who was as tireless in producing memoranda for foreign consumption as in preparing drafts on economic matters and internal politics. During the war his main contact was through the Swedish bankers Wallenberg. His principal efforts were made between November, 1942, and November, 1943. Once again they were directed primarily to making sure of the Allied attitude in the event of an uprising and the establishment of a non-Nazi government. Once, in November, 1942, J. Wallenberg did remark to Goerdeler that the *coup d'état* should be risked even without the British promise of a moderate peace. But this advance assurance was not the only goal. In May, 1943, Goerdeler explained personally to his friends in Stockholm and recorded in a memorandum the territorial terms which he thought might be obtained for Germany, revealing less optimism than Hassell regarding the German-Polish frontier. He also, however, repeatedly stressed a preparedness to make good the wrong that had been done and to democratise Germany. But in the main he developed his plans for a European community to which we shall return. As he was expecting the internal revolt in Germany in September, 1943, he asked some weeks later, again through J. Wallenberg, that the R.A.F. should spare Berlin, Leipzig and Stuttgart until the middle of October "as the oppositional movement has its centres there and the interruption of communications would make the putsch more difficult". All this was passed to the British, but provoked no response and none of these actions brought about direct contact with the West. Some of them, however, are clearly delineated and afford insight into the attitude and motives of the opposing side.

One of the earliest direct steps is associated with the name of the Cecil Rhodes scholar von Trott zu Solz whom we have already got to know for his early oppositional activity and as a member of the Kreisau circle. He was the son of a Prussian Minister of Education, and grandson of von Schweinitz who had been an ambassador in Bismarck's time and of an American grandmother who had been a granddaughter of John Jay, the first Chief Justice of the American Supreme Court. Thus, like Moltke, Trott had a partly Anglo-Saxon family background and also like Moltke formed a link between the aristocrats and Socialist groups of the Opposition. He was a close friend of Kleist-Schmenzin, Leuschner and later of Leber. Hegel's political philosophy and its relation to International Law occupied him as intensively as Marx's social doctrine. Trott spent some time in China working on Far Eastern problems and thereby came in close contact with American circles. He then entered the German Foreign Office with the deliberate intention of using the position as a cover for his oppositional activities.

As we have mentioned, Trott was in London in the summer of 1939. At that time he took part in attempts to inform English circles about the German Resistance and to win them over to a moral alliance. Although he found Chamberlain's reaction to his efforts "icy", he had many English friends, some of them in official circles. Despite the blockade he succeeded in reaching the United States in October, 1939. The declared object of his journey was to take part in a Conference at the American Institute of Pacific Relations. But for the Foreign Office (Weizsäcker?) to send him in wartime to the U.S.A. as an expert on Far Eastern affairs was obviously only a camouflage for a very different mission. His real object Trott defined in a talk with the editor of the *Washington Post*, Felix Morley, as preparing in America a receptive attitude to the great change which in his opinion was about to take place in Germany. The main task was to ensure that the programme of a war of destruction did not compel all those elements to join the National Socialists who had begun to co-operate for the overthrow of Hitler. Thus he saw it as his goal to reserve the increasing tendency to equate Germany with the Nazi régime and so to prepare the way for a timely and reasonable peace.

Trott had a number of conversations along these lines. He informed at least one high official in the State Department and other politically influential people about the men and the objectives of the German underground movement. It is impossible to confirm with certainty whether he really was, as has been claimed, in a position to formulate definite conditions on the basis of which the Opposition hoped to end the war after the overthrow of Hitler and to give a promise that the principal Nazi leaders would be prosecuted for common crimes. The memorandum in which he finally summarised his efforts had a more general scope. It recommended an early clarification of war aims in order to reassure the Opposition and neutralise Nazi propaganda.

Trott supported this suggestion by referring to a psychological fact which was working against the discontent and indignation at Hitler's tyranny: the German people, he said, faced the inescapable dilemma of having to support the régime in war as long as it seemed to be the Allies' intention to destroy Germany. It was therefore important to state clearly that the continuation of National Socialist control was the main obstacle to peaceful existence and that through the overthrow of the régime a tolerable position could be assured for Germany in a new Europe. If, however, the Western powers failed to take up a constructive line there was, in Trott's opinion, the urgent danger of a national Bolshevism which would not halt at the German frontiers. So far, as he correctly said, the war had been conducted without any "frenzy of passion". Neither the British nor the French were fighting for "glory"' or "prestige" or "national grandeur"; they were defending their personal freedom and the principles of Western civilisation. Trott found, however, that this rational attitude was threatened by increasing sacrifices. Therefore a clear goal was needed that had enough emotional and rational attraction to justify the terrible sacrifices demanded. . . . It was urgently necessary, he wrote, to tell the peoples not only why they must fight, but also what they were fighting for.

Trott completed this general suggestion with more detailed proposals. It should be possible, he wrote, for the Allies to lay down certain maximum concessions which would be demanded of the Germans or to guarantee that the territorial status (i.e. of Versailles) should in no circumstances be questioned. Beyond this, certain minimal obligations should be considered on the Allied side in regard to economic concessions and general conditions which would allow Germany to take part in future peaceful co-operation in Europe. The prior obligations devolving upon Germany should not, he declared, consist merely in the overthrow of the present régime, but in the guarantee of post-Hitlerite Germany's honest and active co-operation in a system of peace. Trott recognised that to provide this guarantee changes were needed in the social, economic and political structure of Germany and that these required special discussion. Above all he declared bluntly that Germany must be placed in a position which fulfilled the wishes of all European peoples by excluding the possibility of new wars between them.

In the framework of this constructive programme Trott's memorandum allotted an important role to the United States. He was well aware that a formal act of mediation or a mutual exchange of guarantees was out of the question. But he believed it possible to bring "the moral weight" of the U.S.A. to bear on the European situation. If it was felt throughout Europe, in Allied countries as well as in Germany, that the authority of the United States was behind the efforts to achieve a just and lasting peace, that would assist enormously in furthering constructive processes of thought. Trott was so hopeful that he asked the question : could the Allies not agree among themselves and then solemnly declare to the America people and their Government "that they will fight for and stick by their declared war aims".

In discussing this memorandum we must bear in mind that hostilities had begun only two months previously and that Nazi Germany and Soviet Russia were at that time allies. During the so-called "Sitzkrieg" a return to reason still seemed possible. Apparently the desire for a positive conception of Germany's and Europe's future was the kernel of Trott's proposals. In his opinion such a prospect would decisively strengthen the German Opposition by giving the lie to Hitler's propaganda about the "war of destruction against Germany". All sane and reasonable elements would then combine against the nihilistic and destructive forces in Europe. It is not known to what extent Trott entered in his personal commentaries into the changes which he considered necessary in the reconstruction of Germany apart from the restoration of the Versailles frontiers. And there is only a rough indication of the answer he received. It must suffice to quote some sentences from Mr. Alexander B. Maley's conclusion : "Von Trott's efforts were reinforced by other prominent refugees, including Dr. Heinrich Brüning, Catholic pre-Nazi German Chancellor, who visited the White House for this purpose in December, 1939. President Roosevelt at first showed interest in the appeal to support the German underground, but soon, apparently on the advice of men close to him, discouraged further contacts. Von Trott was even denounced as a Nazi agent, which is bitterly ironical in view of the sequel."

Thus the initiative of this "noble and idealistic young German", as F. Morley calls him, only resulted in supplying Washington with considerable insight into the internal situation in Germany. In every other respect Trott's efforts failed completely. Whatever may be thought of the practical value and feasibility of his proposals, the refusal to show even the most modest degree of sympathy with the German Resistance was very clear and represented a discouraging precedent. Trott returned via Japan to Germany where he continued his underground activity. He ended on the gallows in August, 1944.

Despite this failure, the Opposition made a fresh attempt in November, 1941, to create some form of direct contact with the United States. Peace, though an uncertain peace, still existed between the two countries. This time, efforts were directed towards achieving permanent contact. As intermediary the conspirators selected the American correspondent in Berlin who probably knew more about the real situation than any other Press representative (certainly more than Mr. William L. Shirer). This was Louis P. Lochner who for many years had run the Berlin office of the Associated Press. Having previously attended meetings of oppositional elements, he was taken one night to meet "twelve to fifteen idealistic men", as he has called them. The group consisted of representatives of the federation of the free trade unions and of the Christian trade unions, of the Confessing Church, the former Centre Party, the Democratic Party, the Social Democrats and the German People's Party. In addition, one representative each of Admiral Canaris and Colonel-General Beck were present. It hardly needs to be added that the composition of the group provides interesting evidence of the extent as well as of the cohesion of the Opposition and is well calculated to confirm what has been deduced from other sources of information in this respect.

The meeting took place in the house of Dr. Joseph Wirmer, a former Centre deputy, who has already been mentioned. Jakob Kaiser struck Mr. Lochner as the leading figure of the circle. All present were agreed that America would shortly find herself at war with Germany. They were also agreed on the power of the United States and on the enormous influence which America would have on all decisions. In the course of a discussion on the type of government which was to replace the totalitarian régime Mr. Lochner was asked to make all possible efforts after his return to inform President Roosevelt personally of the movement within Germany to overthrow the Nazi tyranny and to persuade him to answer the question: what sort of political system would appear acceptable in Germany? Mr. Lochner was even given a "secret code" to make direct radio communication possible between the American President and the conspirators.

Like other correspondents, the head of the Associated Press was interned for a while after the outbreak of war. On his return to Washington in June, 1942, he tried of course to fulfil the mission which had been entrusted to him. After several attempts to be received by the President had failed he repeated his request in writing and gave precise reasons why he desired a personal inter-view. The answer he received was negative : he was asked to abandon his request because of its "most embarrassing nature". It took Mr. Lochner some time until he realised on the basis of his other impressions in Washington that this refusal was not acci-dental but was dictated by official policy. The underlying attitude not only excluded every form of encouragement or advice for which the men of the German Opposition were asking : it not only made official contact with the Berlin centre of Resistance impossible, but apparently from the point of view of Washington the mere recognition of the fact that oppositional elements existed in Germany which were able and ready to take over the govern-ment as well as the offer of authentic information concerning this fact were felt to be "most embarrassing".

The third attempt to achieve a direct understanding or at least the basis for a certain degree of co-operation also ended in failure. We have already mentioned the meeting which the Bishop of Chichester had in May, 1942, with two German pastors in Stockholm. His first visitor was Dr. Hans Schönfeld who worked for the World Council of Churches and also for the Foreign Affairs Department of the Evangelical Church in Germany which brought him into close contact with Gerstenmaier. There was not the least doubt of the genuineness of his opposition to the régime; it was attested by all who stood close to him, and by Dulles who later worked with him in Switzerland. If he came on anyone's behalf, he represented the Kreisau circle which had just had its first meeting. The Bishop of Chichester knew that he stood with him on sure and common ground.

The Bishop was even more certain of his second visitor, Dietrich Bonhoeffer, who had been pastor of the German Church in London and whom he knew from those days. He also knew that throughout the years Bonhoeffer had worked zealously with the Council of Brethren of the Confessing Church. The son of a leading German psychiatrist, Bonhoeffer had been principal of a clandestine theological seminary and had also been engaged in widespread political activity. There was not the least doubt of his unyielding attitude. The Bishop knew of Bonhoeffer's words at a meeting of the Opposition when a postponement was suggested in order not to make a martyr of Hitler. As we have already men-tioned in another context, Bonhoeffer said, "If we claim to be Christians we must give no room to tactical considerations." He added: "Hitler is the Anti-Christ. We must therefore continue with our work and root him out whether or not he is successful."

Thus Bonhoeffer represented in the clearest and purest form that type of resistance which did not hesitate to apply a radical solution to the moral dilemma—a dilemma which, as we have said, did not weigh on the conscience of oppositional elements in other countries in any remotely comparable manner. A further statement of Bonhoeffer has been reported which makes this completely clear. At a secret Church conference in Geneva in 1941 he said: "I pray for the defeat of my Fatherland. Only through a defeat can we atone for the terrible crimes which we have committed against Europe and the world." It is not surprising that a man of such convictions—like the other members of the Bonhoeffer family, his brother Klaus and his brothers-in-law Schleicher and Dohnanyi—stood particularly close to Oster. When Dietrich Bonhoeffer went to Stockholm he was furnished with papers which the Intelligence had prepared for him. He had spiritual as well as official authority for his mission.

All the more the Bishop was impressed by the fact that both pastors said materially the same thing, though neither knew of the other's coming. First, Schöfeld informed him of the strength and composition of the oppositional groups, of their progress in organisation and preparation during the last six months. Their purpose, he said, was the elimination of the entire Nazi system including Hitler, Himmler, Goering and Goebbels and the heads of the Gestapo, the SS and the SA. A new government was to be formed in which all oppositional groups would be represented. Their programme, of which he gave the Bishop a written note, envisaged: (1) a considerably decentralised Germany governed according to the dictates of "law and social justice"; (2) economic reconstruction "on truly Socialist principles instead of those of a self-sufficient autarky" as well as close co-operation between free peoples whose mutual dependence would prove to be "the strongest possible guarantee against a relapse into a reactionary European militarism"; (3) a European federation of free states, including a free Polish and a free Czech nation. The federation should be provided with a "common executive organ" under whose authority a "European army for the continual preservation of European security" should be founded.

It is evident from this programme that Schönfeld at least tried to speak for the Opposition as a whole. His statements show very clear similarities with the ideas of the Kreisau circle and, to a certain extent, with Goerdeler's. It also certainly corresponded to the general conviction of most German opponents when Schön-feld came to the conclusion : "The basic principles of national and social life within this federation of free European peoples should be oriented or re-oriented according to the fundamental articles of Christian Faith and life."

With Bonhoeffer the Bishop had a more intimate conversation. He received information about the chief conspirators, their character and their political intentions which inspired him with the fullest confidence and which, one may add, were completely accurate. This was followed by a talk in which Schönfeld joined. Apparently, Bonhoeffer dissociated himself to some extent from Schön-feld's attempt to ensure certain minimal conditions for Germany on the basis of their common attitude. He opposed the possibility of too easy a way out : "We would not be worthy of such a solution. We do not wish to escape repentance. Our action must be under-stood as an act of repentance." Apparently this statement which the Bishop underlined (and which Schönfeld also accepted) con-vinced him most strongly of the honesty of this alliance. It was further suggested that Allied troops would have to occupy Berlin. Though warning against exaggerated hopes and stressing that the Americans and the Russians would have to have a voice in the matter the Bishop declared himself willing to transmit the message.

The crux had been defined by Schönfeld who stated that it was a matter of extreme urgency to know "whether the attitude of the Allies to a Germany that had freed itself from Hitler would differ from that towards a Germany under Hitler. Otherwise there would only be further destruction, chaos and a nihilism that would continually increase as the war proceeded." The Bishop himself summarised the message in two questions : "(1) Would the Allied Governments, once the whole Hitler régime was overthrown, be willing to treat with a bona fide German Government for such a peace settlement as that described . . . including the withdrawal of all German forces from occupied countries, and reparation for damage, and to say so privately to an authorised representative of the German Opposition?—or (2) Could the Allies make a public announcement in the clearest terms to a similar effect?"

After his return to London the Bishop submitted a detailed report and Schönfeld's written notes to Anthony Eden. He received the reply that some of the names mentioned by Bonhoeffer were known to the Foreign Office and that other communications or peace feelers had reached London through other neutral countries. Eden further stated that one must avoid even seeming to negotiate without the participation of the Americans and the Russians, but that he would consider the matter. There followed some correspondence between the Bishop and the Foreign Secretary which has only recently become known. Eden did not doubt the honest conviction of the two pastors. But he thought that the Resistance movement in Germany had so far given little proof that it existed. It must first follow the example of the other oppressed peoples of Europe and take active steps. In vain the Bishop objected that the other peoples had been promised liberation by the Allies, but the Germans had not. The matter rested with Anthony Eden's statement on 17th July that a reply would not be in the "national" interest.

It is not the purpose of this study to enter into an exhaustive discussion of the purely negative attitude which was maintained by the Western Allies throughout the war years. Various motives suggest themselves. One of them, a motive of diplomacy, that is, a fear of endangering the great alliance by separate negotiations even of the most non-committal kind emerges clearly enough, though it would not necessarily have involved a policy of "no action". Moreover such a viewpoint cannot be applied to Trott's initiative in Washington which was undertaken at the time of American neutrality and Nazi-Soviet friendship. Neither do the overtures made through Mr. Lochner which simply sought advice nor those of the two pastors who willingly accepted all the Bishop's reservations point to any German intention of splitting the Allied front. They are evidence rather of the same concern which Trott expressed in his memorandum, the fear of chaos and nihilism. Perhaps this can be understood better today than in the years 1940 and 1942.

Another possible motive of mistrust suggests itself. Must not the somewhat surprising interest which Germans professed for the reconstruction and recuperation of Europe and for a permanent international order have awakened the suspicion that this was a camouflaged "peace offensive" on the part of militarists and nationalists who were trying to consolidate some of Hitler's gains before it was too late? Now it is certainly correct that in the early years von Hassell and Goerdeler were still under some illusions as to attainable national aims though apparently this did not at all embarrass the British who were also arguing from a national point of view. We have mentioned Hassell's memorandum of February, 1940, which was transmitted to Halifax. According to this, the union of Austria and the Sudetenland with the Reich was to remain "outside the discussion" and while Versailles was to be accepted in the West, the German-Polish frontier was to conform substantially to the Reich frontier of 1914. In a suggestion which Hassell appears to have addressed to Washington in the autumn of 1941 the claim to the Sudetenland was dropped. For a settlement of the Corridor problem Hassell now suggested an exchange of territory which would give Poland access to the sea by the incorporation of four eastern districts of East Prussia. It is known that as late as March, 1943, Goerdeler, though thinking that the chance to acquire colonies had been "missed" at that time, believed that South Tyrol could still be recovered besides Austria and the Sudetenland being retained within the Reich.

On the other hand it has been shown that as early as October, 1939, von Trott suggested no more than a guarantee of the Versailles frontiers (in East and West). It may have come as a surprise when he added in his memorandum that "nationalism of the kind which finds its extreme expression in Nazism has definitely been on the decline in Europe for some time". This seems a paradoxical contention, but it makes complete sense if one remembers that, despite its criticism of the political conceptions of the nineteenth century, the Hitler movement represented in many respects only the belated culmination and the morbid exaggeration of that period of secularisation and nationalisation. The truth of the assertion that some of these tendencies were in fact on the wane can be attested by anyone who before 1933 was in touch with the truly progressive, neo-Conservative and Socialist forces which were working for differently based forms of international co-operation in Central Europe. In an as yet unpublished memorandum of November, 1943, in which he defined his attitude to the "six peace points of the American Church Alliance", Trott stressed that such a change was "in keeping with developments at least in Europe, in so far as the concept of the 'National State' is undergoing a profound change which has been hastened by the totalitarian State in that this has overstretched and inwardly undermined the idea of the national State in the old sense, i.e. the ideal based on a 'nation-State' or maximum uniformity in population and language". He supported the principle of cultural autonomy and the restriction of national sovereignty. And in the same memorandum he professed to see the most essential and direct contribution "to the achievement of peace on the Christian side" in the fight against "malignant forces", in the replacement of mass existence by a social order with a Christian orientation and in the formation of Christian individuals.

In the statements which he made in Washington Trott sought to justify his view of the descending curve of nationalism with more concrete evidence. He referred to the fact that Hitler had been obliged to smuggle in the war "through the back door" and that in the years 1938–39 the German people certainly showed as little enthusiasm for war as any other nation. And quite certainly there was nothing "nationalistic" or "militaristic" in the plans of the Kreisau circle for whom Trott was the mouthpiece in foreign affairs. And such a charge could hardly be levelled at Bonhoeffer, the go-between of the Intelligence, who had insisted on a declaration of guilt and an act of penance. And it was known in London and probably also in Washington how little the attitude of soldiers like Beck or of diplomats like Weizsäcker had in common in 1938 with a conventional conception of militarism and nationalism.

To this extent, therefore, the historian will be justified in precisely reversing the charge. The objections which Anthony Eden raised were dictated by understandable considerations, but ones which were confined to purely "national interests". Whether the attitude was so "national" and so tied to thoughts of national sovereignty that embarrassment at the "treason" of the German negotiators still played a part may be left an open question. At any rate, blindness was shown to the manifestation of convictions which had already become rare in the nineteenth century, convictions which sought to bridge national frontiers and warring camps and which paid allegiance not only to national, but to widely framed universal goals.

It is also true of Goerdeler's plans (part of which, incidentally, did not reach London until 1943) that they went far beyond national concepts. His previously mentioned "World Peace Programme" of 1939 was only a first instance. The whole conception of a decentralised and federalistic Germany as well as of a State with a co-operative structure meant a break with the tenets of the nineteenth century and basically also a renunciation of the idea of political sovereignty such as was shared by almost all groups of the German Opposition. Such views were the basis of a memorandum written by Goerdeler in May, 1943, which he transmitted to London through the Wallenbergs and which traced the essentials of a "European community". A "peace plan" probably intended for British readers stated that inter-European frontiers would play an ever-smaller part in the European confederation. Together with a federally organised Germany a number of other unions or federations were proposed for Europe: an East European confederation (Poland, Lithuania, Latvia, Estonia), a South European, a Balkan, a Scandinavian confederation and so on. Goerdeler's thoughts continued clearly in the direction of a European union as a component of a world confederation of nations. In this framework Europe was to approach a state of economic unity protected by police forces drawn from the whole of the continent. For the European confederation a President was proposed elected by the Council every four years from among the Heads of States. The Council was to consist of two representatives from each of the member States. In addition there was a Federal Assembly to which the individual unions should each send five to ten representatives. Similarly, the "World Confederation of Nations" was to be organised not by the States, but by the larger units of which Europe was to be one.

It is not the details of these proposals which interest us here, but the views which they represent. No one can deny that an inter-European body of thought existed in the German Opposition which, whatever its practical feasability, is worthy of all respect. These were men who were ready to contribute to the security of Europe and the world by a basic renunciation of a dangerous-seeming concentration of power in the middle of the continent. To many of them even the dissolution of Prussia seemed part of the sacrifice demanded of them for the sake of an international community. By no stretch of the imagination can such ideas be characterised as concealed nationalism or as an indirect means of achieving a European hegemony. Neither were they thrown up under the pressure of extreme necessity. Rather, ideas of this kind grew from genuine German traditions of the pre-Hitler years.

One can certainly appreciate that Foreign Office officials in the Allied camp felt little inclination to concern themselves in wartime with sweeping plans emanating from the opposite camp in

which, moreover, as yet a radical consequence seemed barely to
be drawn from the German defeat which was steadily becoming
more apparent. But apparently this abstinence was also connected with the fact that it would indeed be "most embarrassing"
even to consider the possibility of an original German contribution to a lasting peace or to contemplate negotiations of any kind
with a bona fide representative from the German side. That
would have meant a complete reversal of the propaganda which
was increasingly insisting on the equation of Nazis with Germans
and in particular was hammering home the theme that German
military leaders ("militarists") who undoubtedly formed a part of
the Opposition were no less execrable than the Hitlerites. Moreover, the recognition, even though at the moment only theoretical,
of an opposite number in negotiation might have entailed moral
obligations reminiscent of the "Pre-Armistice Agreement" of 1918.

At this point a further motive appears which seems to have
strongly influenced the negative attitude of the Western powers.
It was not only their intention to make the clearest object-lesson
of Germany's defeat and to force the High Command itself to
sign the capitulation. As the attitude of Beck and von Witzleben
shows, it would not have been difficult to enforce this demand.
But beyond that they intended to avoid any obligation which
might justify later revisionist claims on the part of the Germans
or which might give a future demagogic rabble-rouser an opportunity to accuse the Allies of cheating. Obviously it was much
better to incur no obligations of any kind. In view of one of the
historical lessons which the failure of Versailles seemed to teach
and of the oblivion into which other "lessons" had fallen, one can
very well understand this process of thought. But rigid adherence
to it led to a self-contradictory policy.

A prelude to this result appeared in the tragedy of the Atlantic
Charter. It was proclaimed on 14th August, 1941, and promised
a policy—without, however, entering into any detailed obligations
—which would, firstly, "seek no aggrandisement, territorial or
other", secondly, would abstain from "territorial changes that do
not accord with the freely expressed wishes of the peoples concerned", and, thirdly, recognised the right of all peoples to choose
their own form of government. It talked of the rights "of all
peoples", "all nations" or "all the men in all the lands". On this
universal basis the United Nations met in January, 1942. Yet, as
Winston Churchill stressed, the Atlantic Charter was not intended

to include obligations of any kind towards enemy countries. This interpretation gives clear expression to the dilemma created by the policy of non-commitment. No one would have admitted at that time (though Stalin was soon to make it clear) that occupied countries (like the Baltic States) or allies (like Poland) could be threatened by annexation or a policy of aggrandisement. Neutral States in any case required no promises. But if the enemy countries were excluded, to whom did the promises in the Atlantic Charter refer? By that exclusion the document was in fact robbed of its main content long before its ideals vanished into the lumber-room of melancholy historical memories.

Whatever may have been the relative weight of the different motives determining the political attitude of the Allies towards the German Opposition, it is clear that all approaches and peace feelers were condemned to failure. Their fate was, as it were, finally sealed and confirmed when the formula of "unconditional surrender" was officially agreed at Casablanca on 24th January, 1943. We must now turn to the significance and consequences of this fact.

2. *"Unconditional Surrender"*

Among the many actors and observers of the contemporary scene to whom the formula of Casablanca was and is a stumbling-block few had such obvious cause for complaint as the head of the American Intelligence on the European Continent, Allen Welsh Dulles. As we have mentioned, he arrived in Switzerland in November, 1942. One of his main tasks was to explore the situation in Germany and to obtain all possible insight into the work of the anti-Nazis and of the underground movement beyond the Swiss frontiers. Undoubtedly Mr. Dulles performed excellent work. He not only succeeded in contacting well-informed political refugees, members of the World Alliance of Churches and occasional travellers from Germany. He also established close contact with active members of the conspiracy itself, primarily with Gisevius, but also with Waetjen, Strünk and through an intermediary with von Trott. In his coded telegrams he gave detailed information about the "Breakers", as he called the conspirators. With the assistance of G. v. S. Gaevernitz he gave Washington full information about the internal situation in Germany and he was even able to send a report one week before 20th July predicting "dramatic developments" in some detail.

It may be asked what effect these very unusual reports had on Allied policy. The American historian Harold C. Deutsch has answered this question by giving it the drastic form : "In which Washington waste-basket did these reports end their existence?" Naturally Mr. Dulles speaks of the official silence with greater reserve, however much it must have disappointed him. But he makes no attempt to conceal his opinion that the Casablanca formula led to a "freeze-up" of Allied policy. In fact, the declaration of January, 1943, not only provided Dr. Goebbels with excellent propaganda weapons (as he himself noted in his diary), but it also robbed Mr. Dulles of effective means of psychological warfare, and this at a time when the Russians were deliberately playing up the distinction between Germans and Nazis, for instance, in declarations by Stalin and by the so-called "National Committee of Free Germany" to which we shall return later. Mr. Dulles notes with regret that while at the end of May and the beginning of July Churchill and Attlee addressed some sort of appeal, though a non-committal one, to the German Opposition, Washington shrouded itself in total silence.

This complaint, however, lies entirely in the framework of tactical considerations; it deplores the negative propaganda value of the Casablanca formula. In the same way, the military criticism expressed in General Eisenhower's entourage was of an exclusively technical character. "After all, no surrender was ever made without some conditions", noted Captain Harry C. Butcher in his diary. In a later entry he added : "There is a feeling that at Casablanca the President and the Prime Minister, more likely the former, seized on Grant's famous terms without realising the full implications to the enemy. . . . Our psychological experts believe we would be wiser if we created a mood of acceptance of surrender in the German Army." Indeed, no expert psychological training was required for this assumption and the technical error of Casablanca coupled with the lack of pliability which resulted from the "freeze-up" may well have considerably delayed total victory and the end of the war. From the same tactical point of view, the policy of unconditional surrender certainly made it harder for the German Opposition to win over recalcitrant generals.

But the problem which concerns us here had quite a different dimension of depth than that of purely tactical considerations. It touches very basic questions and only if that is understood can it be realised what the "freeze-up" of Allied policy meant for the German Opposition to Hitler and for the fate of Europe as a whole. It may well be that the Casablanca formula was intended primarily to strengthen Allied morale and instil fresh energy into the Coalition or to pacify the Russians from whose point of view the campaign in Africa represented only a token "second front". And it can be taken as certain that it did not originally include definite war aims or the decision to impose a Punic peace. It was not until the series of conferences in 1943, from the Washington Conference in May ("Trident"), the Quebec Conference in August ("Quadrant"), to the Moscow Conference in October and Teheran in December that a start was made with filling out the formal framework of an unconditional surrender. And the Morgenthau Plan which proposed turning the industrial heart of Europe into a mainly pastoral and agricultural economy was only officially signed in Quebec in September, 1944. Even then, Winston Churchill was reluctant to support this "act of madness" as he himself has called it, and in a conversation with the Secretary of War soon afterwards President Roosevelt admitted that "he did not know how he had initialled that particular language in the Quebec agreement". It must have happened, he added, "without much thought". But though, as Harry Hopkins frequently noticed, Roosevelt was harassed by the spectre of Woodrow Wilson and sought above all at Casablanca to avoid repeating the mistake of making definite promises which the enemy might one day invoke, the result was paradoxical in that he thereby embarked on a set course which could give rise to the most immoderate and radical demands for punishment. Thus basically Casablanca merely made final that negative attitude which we have already observed and which—in so far as it concerned principles—was destined to disencumber the dictatorial power of the victors of any and every obligation. The refusal to recognise any German negotiator pointed logically to a vacuum. In fact, this extreme consequence was only avoided in the case of Japan by the abandonment of the "condition of unconditional surrender". But with Germany the policy of incurring no prior obligations was retained and it led to the completest imaginable military triumph. But just as this policy had defeated the idealism of the Atlantic Charter, it finally defeated itself by, paradoxically again, leading to the most serious commitments. As a German Government, whatever its composition, would have no other task than to capitulate unconditionally, all responsibility, in fact an unconditional responsibility, redounded on the Allies. With his unerring moral sense, Victor Gollancz defined this result as follows : "The Germans were required to place themselves entirely in our hands. . . . If that does not impose a special obligation on a nation that calls itself civilised, what does?" This characterised the circle to which the policy of unconditional surrender has led : in an attempt to avoid all obligation, obligations of the most categorical kind had been incurred.

It is obvious, of course, that no dealings were possible with a Nazi or a Nazi-appointed Government and one might think that this fact would have given all the greater importance to the German Opposition, not only for the purposes of propaganda or psychological warfare, but in the framework of constructive policy. But instead, as an American has aptly expressed it, the fatality occurred "that the Allied leaders, like their Nazi opponents, became victims of their own war propaganda which insisted that all Germans were in the same boat". Indeed, it even came about (or one might say, a bitter irony of history ensured) that the Western Powers found themselves co-operating with Hitler— not only with his reproaches at the "ambitious clique" of conspirators, but in the last resort with the nihilism of a despiser of the German people who deliberately aimed to bequeath the maximum of destruction and chaos. The same Western powers who had the honest desire to perform democratic educational work found themselves in the confusing and paradoxical situation of inheriting a dictatorial régime and many of its arbitrary methods.

The Allied attitude to the German Opposition is only a part of this broad complex of problems, but a very symptomatic part. When Winston Churchill stated in the House of Commons on 2nd August, 1944, that the events of 20th July were concerned purely with a war of extermination among the dignitaries of the Third Reich, he spoke as much against his better knowledge and aligned himself as much with Hitler and Goebbels as did the U.S. propaganda agencies. Such an attitude was bound to lead to serious set-backs and in the long run it was not in fact the existence, but rather the absence of an anti-Nazi shadow government which would prove to be "most embarrassing". Certainly, many of its original members had meanwhile been killed, but as long as the doctrine continued to be preached to the occupation forces that no German was trustworthy—and despite widespread know-

K

ledge to the contrary, this remained the official thesis for many months—it was extremely difficult to bring the positive forces to bear which had gathered in the German Opposition. There seems therefore some justification for saying a good many unnecessary problems were created by the negative attitude which found classical expression in the formula of unconditional surrender.

At the same time it is clear that Casablanca destroyed any hope of a tolerable peace which might still have been entertained by the German Resistance movement and that therefore any contacts with the West undertaken with this aim could only have questionable value. Before this time and up to the year 1944 there is simply no evidence that the conspirators sought to split the Allied front, as was suspected in London and Washington. But now it seemed as though their own ranks would split into a Western and an Eastern group. After a meeting with von Trott, Gaevernitz reported the former's concern at the "co-ordinated Communist activity" in Germany and at the rapid "slide towards the extreme Left". According to Gaevernitz, Trott had said: "Constructive thoughts and plans for the postwar reconstruction of Germany are coming steadily from the Russian side, while the democratic countries make no proposals whatever concerning the future of Central Europe. Socialist leaders in Germany stress the necessity of filling this vacuum as quickly as possible. If it is allowed to continue, German labour leaders fear that, despite their military victory, the democracies will lose the peace and that the present dictatorship in Central Europe will merely be exchanged for a new one."

This analysis of April, 1944, sounds a note of complete honesty and warning prophecy, but shows rather a fear of being abandoned than a decisive turning to the East. Trott therefore added practical suggestions as to how the democracies could increase their influence on the German workers. As we have already shown, the conspiracy on the whole, including its trade union and even its radical elements, was undoubtedly "Western" in the political sense of the word. It has also been mentioned that at the end of 1942 some of the Socialist members pronounced against action or for its postponement until the Western Allies had landed on the Continent. The overthrow of the Government was not intended to entail conquest by Russia and a Communist inundation of all Europe. If it had to come to a capitulation, the military leaders of the Opposition were also naturally in favour of it happening first in the West, if possible with the prospect of maintaining defence in the East or even of conducting it in co-operation with the West. According to a Gestapo report, Stauffenberg, too, is said to have contacted the British in the spring of 1944 and perhaps also the Americans with peace aims akin to Goerdeler's. He apparently still hoped that the invasion would not take place or could be beaten off and that this would be the psychological moment for a new government. Those were illusions, as were Beck's and Goerdeler's thoughts of an armistice in the West and an opening of the front including the landing of Allied paratroops on German key positions, or the even more far-reaching proposals which Gisevius transmitted to Dulles in May, 1944, suggesting Allied landings near Bremen and Hamburg and the occupation of Berlin by three Allied airborne divisions.

These ideas were certainly neither practicable nor likely to be acceptable to the West, but they deserve mention as a sign of readiness for responsible action and for putting an end to the senseless shedding of blood through spontaneous capitulation and therewith also as an indication of decided preference for the West, one might almost say, of a choice of Europe against Asia.

In addition, another line of thought—which still did not indicate the formation of an "Eastern" camp or the splitting of the Opposition—raised the question whether it would be possible to come to a general peace by agreement with Stalin. For this purpose, beside Hassell, Schulenberg was held in readiness as a possible Foreign Minister of a new government. But Trott was also in favour of "pursuing every possibility which offers, however uncertain". And though deeply concerned about the possibility of an understanding between Stalin and Hitler, Hassell was anxious that the Opposition should not leave Russia out of account. "We must bring off this one remaining achievement", he wrote in August, 1943, "of making either the Russians or the Anglo-Americans understand that an intact Germany lies in their interests. It is true that a sound European centre is in the interests of both East and West. I myself prefer the Western game, but would also accept an understanding with Russia . . ." He expressly declared his agreement with Trott in contrast to the "theoretical and moral obligations" of the others. It is clear that both of them planned a tactical game—in the hope of more easily winning over the West to their ideas if the Opposition retained prospects of negotiation with the East. But real discussions on this basis never in fact came about.

It must be added that the approaches from the Soviet side and the propaganda attempts to influence the German Opposition in the sense of a "national" alliance had essentially the same tactical object though in the opposite direction. This applies to the contact which was taken up on Soviet initiative in Stockholm between Peter Kleist, a henchman of Ribbentrop, and a Russian diplomatic intermediary, Clauss. Their meetings took place in December, 1942, and again in June and September, 1943, and were known to Schulenberg, Trott and Hassell. Hitler allowed them to come to nothing. Very revealing of Russian intentions is the way in which Clauss wrote off the undertaking after the successes at Teheran : American offers, he said, had been so generous that Germany could no longer compete. And he added : "The Trojan horse with which Stalin stormed the American citadel was the threat with the 'National Committee of Free Germany'." By the end of 1943, therefore, this organisation had served its purpose.

In fact, the National Committee was essentially intended as a diplomatic weapon. Its propaganda effect at the front was infinitesimal, however skilful the "free" and "national" camouflage may have been. That very fact tended to make it harder for the Communist groups in Germany to adopt this line. There were no contacts with the civil or military leaders of the internal German Opposition, even in the form of indirect influence. Stauffenberg is said to have stated that he did not think much of "proclamations from behind barbed wire" and there is definite evidence that the news of 20th July struck the National Committee "as unexpectedly as a bomb". Just as Kleist's relationship with his Russian contact-man became pointless after Teheran, so significantly the National Committee was no longer mentioned in the Soviet Press throughout the spring and summer of 1944.

In view of all this the exploratory moves of the Opposition towards the East, either in thought or deed, should not be misunderstood as a pro-Soviet orientation. Once again it was Gisevius who misled Dulles in this respect. The American observer indeed noted that in the final result there were no differences of opinion among the conspirators concerning an Eastern or a Western orientation and all were beginning to realise it would have to be "unconditional and simultaneous surrender". But he also claimed that they fell out over the question "whether to look eastwards to Communism or westwards to democracy" and that this threat to their unity continued "to the very last minute". Moreover, he blurs the picture by calling the western group "military" and "revolutionary" and the eastern group "evolutionary". This judgement is clearly caused by overstressing Moltke's thesis that "Hitler and his accomplices must drink the bitter cup of defeat to the dregs before history and the German people". But in reality, as we saw, the Kreisau circle in no way favoured mere inactivity and it was certainly much more "revolutionary", at least in economic and social questions, than the other non-Communist elements of the Opposition. In many respects Moltke and his friends were prepared to take the Soviet experiment very seriously.

The same is known to apply to von Trott. He recorded those political ideas which were most important to him in a memorandum, "Germany between East and West", which has unfortunately been lost. It was probably not confined to expounding Germany's central position in politics and diplomacy, but concentrated on cultural and social matters. In connection therewith Trott is said to have coined the formula that it was a matter of "combining the *Realprinzip* of the East with the *Personalprinzip* of the West". That is exactly the same combination or middle position which has emerged from our discussion of the thought of the Kreisau circle and it certainly goes beyond all tactical considerations. In the earlier mentioned messages which he addressed to Dulles in April, 1944, Trott tried to urge the West to take constructive action by playing up Communist activity and Soviet propaganda in Germany and shortly before the Casablanca Conference he recorded his thoughts in another memorandum also sent direct to Dulles which could not possibly have been interpreted as pro-Soviet. Properly considered, it is still of importance today with its prophecy of decisive developments in the social rather than in the military field and with its hope of a popular movement against a Communist and atheistic dictatorship. We will therefore include some quotations from it here.

Trott started from the disappointing experiences resulting from all discussions with the West. In particular he stressed the inability of the Western powers to understand that the Germans themselves were an oppressed people living in occupied territory and that the Opposition ran the greatest dangers in persisting in its activity. The result was, Trott continued, that "the Opposition sees the Anglo-Saxon countries filled with bourgeois prejudice and Pharisaical theories. There is a strong temptation to turn to the East". The reason for this was belief in "the possibility of fraternisation between the Russian and the German people, though not between their present governments. Both peoples have broken with the bourgeois way of thought, both have suffered deeply, both desire a radical solution of social questions extending beyond national frontiers, both are in the process of returning to the religious, though not to the ecclesiastical traditions of Christianity. The German soldier feels respect, not hatred for the Russian. The Opposition believes that the decisive development in Europe will take place in the social, not the military sphere. If the campaign in Russia reaches a certain stalemate after the German armies have been thrown back a revolutionary situation might result on both sides. Fraternisation between German and imported foreign workers is also an important factor. Hitler has been forced to concern himself with the working class and has helped them to an increasingly strong position; the bourgeoisie, the intellectuals and the generals are becoming less and less important. Hitler will fall and the brotherhood of the oppressed is the basis on which a completely new Europe will be built."

This was the same visionary idea of a "brotherhood of the oppressed" as was sounded in Moltke's thoughts of a restoration of the picture of man and in the connection with Christian groups in other occupied countries. Stauffenberg adhered to it particularly, however narrow the basis for such a hope may have been. Instances of fraternisation with foreign workers were at any rate not lacking, and Stauffenberg's attempts to prevent Russian volunteers serving on the German side from being misused as cannon-fodder and as tools of German or Russian nationalism brings this basic conception into full clarity. Thus it is at this point that once again and in contradiction to all misinterpretations the innermost impulse becomes visible which gives the German Opposition its particular status. It was entirely committed to a stand on principle against every kind of totalitarian system, to a basic insistence on the tenets of European civilisation, on the dignity of man, on the religious traditions of Christianity and the inalienable values of human existence. All this was directed against the anonymous forces of dehumanised social and political systems. In stressing this one must admit, however, that the German Opposition found little support in so-called realities either of the West or of the East. It fought a battle of the European vanguard against hope and with no prospect of direct national or social reward.

This was, in fact, the situation after January, 1943, whatever expedients were tried or desperate efforts undertaken. Basically there was no chance and nothing remained but to do what was necessary. Mr. Dulles summed this up very accurately when he stated: "From Sweden and Switzerland, even from Spain, Turkey and the Vatican the conspirators were told that they could count on no promises of any kind on the part of the Allies, but that if they were prepared to do so, they would have to go ahead, not in the hope of better peace terms, but simply because their duty to put their own house in order was an absolute one. It was not conditional upon the help and promises of others." And in fact, while other underground movements in Europe received plentiful material and psychological support and had very concrete rewards within reach, only the German was entirely dependent on its own resources. These were only super-ficially military, in principle they were of a spiritual and religious nature. On this basis, murder could be considered a moral duty, a duty to clear the German name and free the world from an evil, a liberation which had to be brought about by the Germans themselves. We have quoted von Tresckow's words which clearly express this. In the same sense the former Secretary of State Erwin Planck stated: "The attempt on Hitler's life must be made, if only for the moral rehabilitation of Germany . . . even if thereby no direct improvement of Germany's inter-national prospects is achieved." That was not the attitude of the Opposition in 1938 or at the beginning of the war when it still seemed possible to save parts of the political and social structure of prewar Europe. But Casablanca was finally answered with another "unconditional" attitude—that of attack on a shameful régime, whether or not its overthrow promised a tolerable in-stead of an intolerable peace. In fact, it promised nothing—except a shortening of the war which might save innumerable lives and spare the whole of Europe and of Western culture the deepest decline which was yet to come.

SUMMARY

I N attempting to assess the essentials of the matters discussed here in a kind of balance sheet, one must leave certain questions open, not only questions of fact which will never perhaps be completely clarified, but questions of judgement which transcend the competence of the historian and probably that of mortal man altogether. Accordingly, we neither assume the office of judge nor claim the role of counsel for the prosecution or the defence. Respect for the seriousness and the comprehensive character of the problems involved was, beside many other grounds, reason enough not to undertake this study as a plea for the defence or to consider it as such in any of its phases. Nor is it the historian's task to decide whether and to what degree the extent and characteristics of the German Opposition to Hitler comprised, as it were, mitigating circumstances compared with the sufferings which the Third Reich inflicted upon millions of human beings and with the devastation it bequeathed. Suffice it to remember—and this is perhaps more important than any statement which could be made today from behind a writing desk—that the leading men of the conspiracy themselves, churchmen as well as laymen, amidst trials and the storm of events lived and died for the idea of atonement. In a farewell letter written in prison Goerdeler expressed a line of thought common to many other documents of the German Resistance. He ended the letter with the words : "I ask the world to accept our martyrdom as penance for the German people."

This study was begun twelve years ago not with reference to the metaphysical or political aspect of this plea, but for the sake of historical justice. Its first aim was therefore to clarify facts which at that time were largely unknown to a wider public and even in subsequent years have hardly ever been presented in their variety and mutual relationship. As in every historical study, these facts further require to be placed in a wider context and subjected to repeated critical examination as far as the underlying sources are concerned. All this belongs to the legitimate province of the historian. And in regard to the research of the last decade it can be said that within the purely factual field a comparatively wide area can now be considered secure and removed from the atmosphere of camouflage and ostracism which surrounded it and from the distorting influence which party strife, passion, resentment and political propaganda of every kind inevitably exerted.

Some few results of this process may be summarised here. The German Opposition to Hitler was not only numerically broader than has often been conceded, but was much more widespread than could have been expected under conditions of terror. It not only developed through various stages of non-conformity and non-agreement: from the hostility which was stifled behind prison walls and barbed wire, from the silence of a potential Opposition, from humanitarian protest and secret assistance rendered to victims of persecution to the counter-propaganda of opponents, to underground activity, to a spiritual and religious attack on the basic ideas of all totalitarian systems and to active planning and political resistance. Beyond this it is a fact that the German Opposition was taking shape in various forms long before the war and reached its first climax in an attempt to prevent war. It was not the threat of defeat which spurred it to action; on the contrary, some of its leaders were convinced that the victory of Hitler would be the triumph of the Anti-Christ, "the arch-enemy of the whole world" and thus the greatest of all possible catastrophes. They were convinced of this—and also of the practical impossibility of such an outcome—at a time when to many people a German military victory still seemed entirely possible. While the cutting edge, the "vanguard" of the Opposition was military, as cannot be otherwise under a totalitarian system, its body and soul came from political and ethical considerations. Though the conspiracy was led by men prominent in limited social groups, the rank and file comprised all social elements, bourgeois and military, aristocratic and proletarian, spiritual and lay. It produced a number of individuals who were able and willing to take over the government of Germany in the provinces and towns as well as at the centre. It maintained contact with foreign countries and did not fail to give warning as well as proof of its existence. While for obvious reasons the Opposition could never be a mass movement, it was equipped with a network of cells and here and there may have extended down to small communities. Moreover, it had a concrete programme which, though not binding on all its elements, was

L

accepted by a broad coalition of oppositional forces and extended far beyond merely negative aims.

With the analysis of this positive programme, of the motives and the main ideas of the German Opposition, the historian turns from the establishment to the interpretation of facts and this is, of course, the more important, but also the more difficult part of his task. But here, too, the ground has become considerably firmer. The significance of this for the historical picture of the recent past should not be underestimated, even though fresh strife has meanwhile arisen on this firmer soil concerning, for instance, the practical political content of the programme, its restorationist or revolutionary traits and the basic questions of the Resistance to which we have characterised our attitude in the Foreword and at certain points in the text.

For the sake of perspective and also a certain topical interest it will be as well, therefore, to recall for a moment the scope which distortions and prejudices concerning the phenomenon of the German Opposition assumed around the year 1945. It is undeniable that, after being obliged to admit its existence, Anglo-Saxon statements in particular caricatured it considerably and attacked the "officers" in a manner tantamount almost to co-operation with Hitler. In fact, leading newspapers gave staggering evidence of this strange alliance.

It will suffice to quote from some leading articles explaining the meaning of 20th July to the American public. On 9th August, 1944, the *New York Times* stated that the details of the attempt on Hitler's life were more reminiscent of "the atmosphere of a gangster's lurid underworld" than of what "one would normally expect within an officers' corps and a civilised State". The article noted reproachfully that for a whole year some of the highest officers in the Germany Army had been busying themselves with plans "to capture or kill the Head of State and the Commander-in-Chief of the Army". Finally they carried out their plan "with a bomb, the typical weapon of the underworld". Earlier, on 1st August, the *New York Herald Tribune* had written: "If Hitlerism has begun its last stand by destroying the militarist tradition it has been doing a large part of the Allies' work for them." On 9th August, the same newspaper added the following comment: "American people as a whole will not feel sorry that the bomb spared Hitler for the liquidation of his Generals. Americans hold no brief for aristocrats as such and least of all for those given to

the goosestep and, when it suits their purpose, to collaboration
with low-born, rabble-rousing corporals. Let the Generals kill the
Corporal, or vice versa, preferably both."

There is a considerable difference between the ethics of these
editorials and those of the men—many of them indeed officers and
aristocrats—who conceived it their duty to break the bonds of
accustomed loyalty and "capture or kill" the Head of State. The
problem of militarism should certainly not be taken lightly. But
the bogus theory which has been woven round this historical
phenomenon has entailed intolerable generalisations which simply
cannot be reconciled with the spirit of the German Opposition
movement such as the evidence has revealed. This shows rather
that the traditions of a genuine "Prussian militarism", in so far
as they were still present in Nazi Germany, formed a definite
bulwark against nationalistic and demagogic excesses. It may
even be regretted that not a larger part of these traditions survived the spirit of the times. However that may be, the leading
military and aristocratic members of the conspiracy were certainly not tied to narrow conceptions of their caste or calling, but
thought to a great extent in terms of a restoration of human and
supranational values. Their strongest driving force were moral
and religious impulses. It will be unnecessary to summarise again
here the thoughts and deeds which support this interpretation.

On the other hand, a related aspect must be briefly touched on
in this concluding survey. It concerns the aristocratic and conservative elements or the restorationist tendencies within the German
Opposition and thereby passes from the refutation of old mis-
understandings to the present-day discussion. A purely sociological approach does not go very far to illumine this problem which
has, as we have explained, remarkably little to do with class differences. Neither is it enough to stress the difference in attitude
between successive generations, the difference between those who,
unshaken in their historical thought, adhered to the picture of a
better past, whether of Imperial or of Weimar Germany, and
those who had revolutionary aims. Real as this difference was, it
does not supply the key to understanding. None of the older men
—and certainly not Goerdeler—was reactionary in the sense that
he was not convinced of the necessity of a radically fresh start:
none of the young ones wanted a violent upheaval such as the
Russians had carried out or Hitler encouraged by undermining
all historical structures. Aristocratic, i.e. responsible thought on

political leadership and a conservative idea of freedom were represented in both camps.

Because of certain terminological difficulties it will also be advisable to return here to the starting point of this study in so far as it concerned the refutation of American misinterpretations. It is obvious that for observers in the United States an appreciation of the aristocratic element in the Opposition is rendered difficult by centuries-old democratic and egalitarian traditions and that of the conservative element by a terminology which differs considerably from that customary in Europe. This will only be touched on here in so far as it is important for an appreciation of the German Opposition. Americans writing on this theme with sympathy will be inclined to give the general label of "Liberals" to the most energetic opponents of the Nazis, while in the European sense they may have been radical Socialists or radical Conservatives, at any rate men who fought State tyranny as well as unrestricted individualism. There has, after all, since the days of Edmund Burke, been a freedom movement against tyranny— whether of the old authorities or one exercised in the name of revolutionised masses—that stands under the Conservative banner. Conversely, in the United States this word has become attached to the successors of classical Liberalism who are opposed to all State interference in the personal or the economic sphere. This very nomenclature ought to make it possible to understand, if not to accept as a verdict, that the dividing lines within the German Opposition were of a very different kind. Thus, as we have said, the Kreisau aristocrats in particular and other Conservatives as well as their Socialist friends saw Goerdeler as a "reactionary" because of his "liberal" addiction to the free-trade and bourgeois ideals of the nineteenth century.

This divergence in the use of concepts ought not to confuse the issue, but it gives increased cause to avoid one-sided generalisations. In fact, Liberals, Socialists and Conservatives all took part in the German Opposition in varying admixtures, but all with the basic desire to restore freedom in one way or another. Certainly the Resistance movement cannot be dubbed reactionary because conservative and aristocratic elements contributed to it so considerably. In so far as a restorationist tendency existed in the German Opposition it aimed in part at the renewal of a social and economic system so far as possible free from political intervention in the sense of the bourgeois historical epoch. On the other hand, the desire to "restore" the values of Western culture, that is, human dignity or, in Moltke's words, the "right relationship between responsibility and aspiration" was certainly also central for Goerdeler, but corresponded in a particular degree to Conservative thought. We saw that in the religious sphere orthodoxy was the strongest advocate of the duty to resist. In exactly the same way a genuine political Conservatism regained its traditional opposition to the glorification of State or nation, to the idolisation of technology and Mammon and in fact to everything that makes man a means to an end.

Thus everywhere in Europe, among Catholics and Protestants alike, a revival took place of the forces of a religious, cultural and political Conservatism. In general the approaching wave of nihilism and the threatening devitalisation of a mechanised and secularised social structure summoned strong counter-forces into being. In Germany this had already become apparent in parts of the youth movement and other neo-Conservative groups of the 'twenties. Under the pressure of the Hitler régime these forces combined with Socialist elements to form a front which can hardly be called "Liberal" and which was equally opposed to the centralistic national State, to the social system underlying it and to other nineteenth-century articles of faith.

This meant among other things that the men of the German Opposition had no intention of taking up the idea of a popular State where the Weimar Republic had dropped it. Their plans aimed in varying degrees and shades at a conservative and decentralised democracy with a more or less strong admixture of Socialism. It will be useful to recall that the fathers of the American Republic were also convinced that unrestricted majority rule would certainly lead to tyranny. Their system of checks and balances differed from that of the German Opposition, but it, too, had characteristics of a Conservative democracy and the stress which was laid on local self-government and decentralisation was not so very different in both cases. In Germany this meant a return to sound older traditions, to the thought of Freiherr von Stein, for instance, and it was a challenge to tackle problems which are still very topical today. They are by no means solved by an outward stress on stabilising factors in the ʼdemocratic structure or by a formally very far-reaching federalism. Adam von Trott's words that the decisive development in Europe would take place "in the social, not in the military sphere" have lost none of their importance either through the experiences of the Cold War or through those of "Co-existence".

The same will apply to the international thought of the German Opposition. Here, too, there is a close relation to the most urgent of our present-day needs. It may be noted that their plans for the dissolution of Prussia and the federalisation of Germany were not of a purely negative kind or dictated by resentment; they sought not only to stifle at birth the formation of a power hegemony in the centre of Europe, though after Hitler's excesses they recognised this as a necessary measure and offered it as a sacrifice which Germany had to make if the peoples were to live together in harmony. Beyond this the Opposition thought in terms of an economically unified and viable, but culturally and politically diversified Central Europe organised as a union of federations and integrated into a European and world confederation. But they also knew that, as Moltke had expressed it, all this was "less a problem of frontiers and soldiers, of top-heavy organisations and grandiose plans" than a question of how "the picture of man can be restored in the hearts of our fellow-citizens". In other words, they knew that all reconstruction, national and international, depended on the rehabilitation of human dignity whose estimation had been allowed to fall so low. It was no mere phrase when the conviction of the Opposition was explained to the Bishop of Chichester in these terms: "The foundation principles ... within this federation of free European nations should be orientated or re-orientated towards the fundamental principles of Christian Faith and Life."

It may well be that this "idealism" means little to many modern "neo-realists". As a reaction against misused ideologies, ideological fronts and the crusading character of the last war it has even become customary in certain circles in the United States to look on "military security" and "the national interest" as the quintessence of practical politics and the sole criteria of action. And yet a leading thinker of this school, George F. Kennan, has spoken of the urgent need of men of Graf Moltke's stamp if "the future of the region from the Elbe to the Behring Strait is once again to be a happier one". Perhaps confidence in such forces comes indeed nearer to the innermost kernel of contemporary conflicts than trust in "soldiers and top-heavy organisations". And in this connection particularly it is one of the enduring titles of honour that the German Opposition produced men who on their part in it gave notable testimony to the revolt of the human against the inhuman.

Thereby the tragedy of 20th July gains all the more in historical perspective. It can be taken as certain today that the *Herald Tribune* was in error when it prophesied, "American people as a whole will not feel sorry that the bomb spared Hitler". Agreed, a successful attempt on Hitler's life might possibly have prevented the continuation of a series of brilliant American victories. But instead, life and health would have been preserved to innumerable human beings, to hundreds of thousands of soldiers on all fronts who were killed or maimed between July, 1944, and May, 1945, and to millions of civilians in the liquidation camps of the East or in bombed and burning cities. Moreover, the failure of the attempt led to the elimination of individuals who, with numerous others, left a grievous gap virtually impossible to fill in the forces available for reconstruction.

It is impossible to say today whether nevertheless the seed which they sowed or from which they themselves grew has remained alive despite year-long denigration and despite the temptation of seemingly restored normalcy inherent in the *Wirtschaftswunder*, the miracle of German economic recovery.

At any rate, it was the intention of the National Socialist régime to destroy root and branch the élite of the German Opposition. To understand this fanatical purpose fully one should read Himmler's speech to the Gauleiters of 3rd August, 1944, in which he attempted to back-date the "stab in the back" to the aristocratic Officers' Corps of the first world war. When Isa Vermehren was sent to Buchenwald as a victim of the *Sippenhaft* (i.e. as a relative of one of the conspirators) she met there ten Stauffenbergs and eight Goerdelers. But not all leading members of the Opposition lost their lives, and ideas generated in an extreme situation but related to what is permanently human possess their own dynamism. One may hope that in a country where the roots were laid bare in every conceivable sense and where, in the words of Graf Lehndorff, "everything from the past" was forcibly "torn away", the will to take basic questions seriously will not die out, or to remember the obligations which the example of the Opposition imposes. For that, admittedly, it will be necessary to renounce that cynicism which confuses these ideals with ideological catchwords and itself ends by renouncing all obligatory norms.

But once again and in conclusion it must be stated that the

German Opposition bequeathed ideals which are not bound up with locality or nationality. This gives it its unique character. Though part of a European movement, the German Resistance possessed characteristics which were peculiar to itself and were derived from the particular conditions of life in Germany. Everywhere else—and this is not said for the purpose of generalising criticism—there were undoubtedly asocial and criminal elements among the fighters for freedom who were inclined by nature to "resistance". In the German Opposition the "underworld" of which the *New York Times* spoke was virtually unrepresented. Hitler could use all the thugs himself. Moreover, the German Opposition was in an exceptional position, or approached it increasingly after the outbreak of war, in that the battle for the liberation of the Fatherland was inevitably combined with the prospect of a humiliating defeat. The only way to resolve this conflict was to replace a negative by a positive ideal, by a goal that extended beyond the struggle against the Nazis or against outward oppression and was not attained by the overthrow of the régime and the abolition of tyranny in only one country. Stronger impulses of a purely human character were required which could claim universal validity. Thus the leading men of the German Opposition belonged in a special sense to the vanguard of a new Europe which was to be freed from disruption by nationalism and from alienation through overt or anonymous dictatorship. They were, as has been well said, "much more than merely the opposite poles to Hitler and his baneful system. Beside its significance for the events of our time, their battle was on a higher plane an attempt to overcome spiritually the nineteenth century".

Gräfin Marion Dönhoff who wrote these words summarises very aptly one of the basic aims of many of the men who have been named on these pages and particularly of the members of the Kreisau circle. Their fundamental desire, she says, was "to free man who had become an empty shell, a tool of technology, a creation of abstract political ideas, a function of science, a servant of economic laws which he himself had made absolute—to free him from all prejudices and once more to set up before him the genuine *humanitas*, the true picture of man in his dignity and pride. Only when man has resumed his proper place can there be harmony in the individual and in the State. But that is only possible if man remembers his origins and recalls that he is created in the image of God with all the responsibility that this implies".

SELECT LIST OF
BOOKS IN ENGLISH ON THE GERMAN RESISTANCE

ABSHAGEN, Karl Heinz : *Canaris*. Tr.: Alan Houghton Brodrick. London : Hutchinson, 1956.

ANDREAS-FRIEDRICH, Ruth : *Berlin Underground, 1938-1945*. Tr. : Barrows Mussey. With an introd. note by Joel Sayre. New York: Holt, 1947.

BARTZ, Karl : *The Downfall of the German Secret Service*. With an introd. by Ian Colvin. London: Kimber, 1956.

BETHGE, Eberhard : *The Biography of Dietrich Bonhoeffer*. London: Collins, 1970.

BOVERI, Margret : *Treason in the Twentieth Century*. Transl. from the German. London: Macdonald, 1961.

BRYANS, J. Lonsdale: *Blind Victory*. London: Skeffington, 1951.

CAHEN, Fritz Max : *Men against Hitler*. With an introd. by Wythe Williams. London: Jarrolds, 1939.

COLVIN, Ian : *Admiral Canaris, Chief of Intelligence*. London : Odhams Press, 1954.

DEUTSCH, Harold C. : *The Conspiracy against Hitler in the Twilight War*. Minneapolis: University of Minnesota Press, 1968.

DONOHOE, James J.: *Hitler's Conservative Opponents in Bavaria, 1930-1945*. Leiden : Brill, 1961.

DULLES, Allan Welsh: *Germany's Underground*. New York: Macmillan, 1947.

FITZGIBBON, Constantine : *The Shirt of Nessus*. The Putsch, July 20, 1944. London : Cassell, 1956.

FRAENKEL, Heinrich : *The German People versus Hitler*. London : Allen & Unwin, 1940.

FRAENKEL, Heinrich: *The Other Germany*. London: Drummond, 1942.

GALLIN, Mary Alice : *German Resistance to Hitler: ethical and religious factors*. Washington, D.C.: Catholic Univ. of America Press, 1962.

GISEVIUS, Hans Bernd : *To the Bitter End*. Tr.: Richard and Clara Winston. London : Cape, 1948.

GRAML, Hermann, and others: *The German Resistance to Hitler*. Tr.: Peter and Betty Roff. London : Batsford, 1970. By Hermann Graml, Hans Mommsen, Hans Reichhardt and Ernst Wolf.

HASSELL, Ulrich von : *The von Hassell Diaries, 1939-1944*. Introd. by Allen Welsh Dulles. London : Hamilton, 1948.

JANSEN, Jon, and Stefan Weyl : *The Silent War*. The underground movement in Germany. Foreword by Reinhold Niebuhr. Philadelphia: Lippincott, 1943.

KRAMARZ, Joachim : *Stauffenberg*. The Life and Death of an Officer. Introd. by H. R. Trevor-Roper. London: Deutsch, 1967.

LEBER, Annedore, ed.: *Conscience in Revolt*. Sixty-four stories of resistance in Germany, 1933-45. Tr.: Rosemary O'Neill. Introd. by Robert Birley. London: Vallentine, Mitchell, 1957.

LEND, Evelyn : *The Underground Struggle in Germany*, and *News from Nowhere*. New York: League for industrial democracy, 1938.

LEUNER, H. D.: *When Compassion was a Crime*. Germany's Silent Heroes, 1933-45. London: Oswald Wolff, 1966.

LIEPMANN, Heinz : *Fires Underground*. A narrative of the secret struggle carried on by the illegal organisations in Germany under penalty of death. London: Harrap, 1936.

MANVELL, Roger, and Heinrich Fraenkel : *The July Plot*. The attempt in 1944 on Hitler's life and the men behind it. London: The Bodley Head, 1964.

PRITTIE, Terence : *Germans against Hitler*. Foreword by H. R. Trevor-Roper. London : Hutchinson, 1964.

RITTER, Gerhard : *The German Resistance*. Carl Goerdeler's struggle against tyranny. Tr.: Robert Thomas Clark. London: Allen & Unwin, 1958.

ROTHFELS, Hans : *The Political Legacy of the German Resistance Movement*. Bad Godesberg: Inter Nationes. 1969.

ROYCE, Hans : *Germans against Hitler*. 4th ed. comp. and suppl. by Erich Zimmerman and Hans-Adolf Jacobsen. Tr.: Allan and Lieselotte Yahraes. Bonn: Berte-Verlag, 1960.

SCHLABRENDORFF, Fabian von: *Revolt against Hitler*. The personal account of Fabian von Schlabrendorff. Prepared and ed. by Gero v. S. Gaevernitz. London: Eyre and Spottiswoode, 1948.

SCHLABRENDORFF, Fabian von: *The Secret War against Hitler*. Foreword by Terence Prittie. London: Hodder & Stoughton, 1966.

SCHOLL, Inge: *Six against Tyranny*. Tr.: Cyprus Brooks. London: Murray, 1955.

SCHRAMM, Wilhelm von : *Conspiracy among Generals*. Tr. and ed. by Robert Thomas Clark. London: Allen & Unwin, 1956.

SYKES, Christopher: *Troubled Loyalty*. London: Collins, 1969.

ZELLER, Eberhard : *The Flame of Freedom*. The German Struggle against Hitler. Tr.: R. P. Heller and D. R. Masters. London: Oswald Wolff, 1967.

INDEX

(Date of Death added for Victims of Nazi Terror)